Heather Reeday was born in the Yorkshire Dales and moved to London to begin a career as an air-stewardess. She then formed a tour operating company specialising in holidays in Greece and Cyprus. She is now a freelance travel writer and spends much of her time in Greece, especially the Dodecanese Islands.

She lives in Edgware, Middlesex with her Greek husband.

To my mother

Acknowledgements

I am greatly indebted to the National Tourist Organisation of Greece in Athens and London for their help in gathering the material for this book. I would also like to thank Kyriakos H. Metaxas of The Greek Gazette for allowing me access to his excellent library of Greek literature and all the valuable advice he has so generously given.

Front cover: The mediaeval castle, Lindos, (Rhodes), built on a site that has been occupied continuously since 2,500 BC. Tourists now enjoy the warm waters of the bay which provided safe anchorage for St Paul in the first century AD.

Greek Island Series
Greek Kaleidoscope
Heather Reeday

Roger Lascelles, Cartographic and Travel Publisher
47 York Road, Brentford, Middlesex TW8 0QP Telephone: 01-847 0935

Publication Data

Title	Greek Kaleidoscope
Typeface	Compugraphic Times
Photographs	By courtesy of The Greek Gazette, London; The Greek Tourist Office, London; Cambas Wine Company, Crete; Leonides Lellos, Greece
Printing	Kelso Graphics, Kelso, Scotland
ISBN	0 903909 65 0
Edition	This first: June 1988
Publisher	Roger Lascelles 47 York Road, Brentford, Middlesex, TW8 0QP.
Copyright	Heather Reeday

Distribution

Africa:	South Africa —	Faradawn, Box 17161, Hillbrow 2038
Americas:	Canada —	International Travel Maps & Books, P.O. Box 2290, Vancouver BC V6B 3W5.
	U.S.A. —	Boerum Hill Books, P.O. Box 286, Times Plaza Station, Brooklyn, NY 11217, (718-624-4000)
Asia:	Hong Kong —	The Book Society, G.P.O. Box 7804, Hong Kong 5-241901
	India —	English Book Store, 17-L Connaught Circus/P.O. Box 328, New Delhi 110 001
	Singapore —	Graham Brash Pte Ltd., 36-C Prinsep St.
Australasia:	Australia —	Rex Publications, 413 Pacific Highway, Artarmon NSW 2064. 428 3566
	New Zealand —	David Bateman Ltd. P.O. Box 65602, Mairangi Bay, Auckland 10 (9-444-4680)
Europe:	Belgium —	Brussels - Peuples et Continents
	Germany —	Available through major booksellers with good foreign travel sections
	GB/Ireland —	Available through all booksellers with good foreign travel sections.
	Italy —	Libreria dell'Automobile, Milano
	Netherlands —	Nilsson & Lamm BV, Weesp
	Denmark —	Copenhagen - Arnold Busck, G.E.C. Gad, Boghallen, G.E.C. Gad
	Finland —	Helsinki — Akateeminen Kirjakauppa
	Norway —	Oslo - Arne Gimnes/J.G. Tanum
	Sweden —	Stockholm/Esselte, Akademi Bokhandel, Fritzes, Hedengrens Gothenburg/Gumperts, Esselte Lund/Gleerupska
	Switzerland —	Basel/Bider; Berne/Atlas; Geneve/Artou; Lausanne/Artou; Zurich/Travel Bookshop

Contents

Foreword

It is with unalloyed pleasure that I have undertaken to write a very few lines as a foreword to Heather Reeday's delightful *Greek Kaleidoscope.*

Each of the myriad books written around the Greek theme has its own particular flavour. Miss Reeday has succeeded better than most in capturing the very essence of the country and nowhere more so than in her chapter dealing with the splendidly Greek eccentricities of the highly individualistic George and his decidedly erratic Cretan taverna.

This book will serve as the most entertaining and readable of companions to those visiting Greece for the first time and, indeed, for those veterans who, most happily for us, wish to know us even better.

'Now,' as they say, 'read on.'

P. Analytis
Director, Greek Tourist Office, London.

Introduction

Greece, that mountainous country of the eastern Mediterranean rubbing shoulders with Asia, is surrounded by its many islands, carelessly scattered in the blue waters of the Aegean and Ionian seas.

Viewed from the air, this beautiful country is a mass of mountains dominated by the peaks of Olympus, Parnassus and Helicon. Olympus and Parnassus can be seen from many parts of northern Greece, shimmering and gleaming from the snow that caps them most of the year. Their commanding presence explains their influence over the myths and legends of Greek culture.

Greece is, in fact, one of the most mountainous countries in Europe; tangled ranges cover some four-fifths of the land surface. In many parts of the country, the mountains drop down to the sea, and the awe-inspiring view as you approach them from the Mediterranean is one of an extraordinary coalescence, a natural fusion of mountain and sea. The great backbone of mountains which run from the centre to the south of the Peloponnese is called the Pindus range in the north, and gathers many names as it runs southwards. It ends with the five-fingered Pentadaktylon range, running into the sea at Cape Matapan.

Climatically Greece is governed by two factors, the mountains and the sea. The weather can be very cold in winter and extremely hot in summer. The spring is short but usually warm and the countryside is a beautiful tapestry of wild flowers.

The personality and scenery of the islands vary considerably, from the green and fertile island of Samos to the harsh bare rocks of the Cyclades. There is Thassos with its forests and summer rain-storms and Rhodes with its lush, vine-covered valleys and scented pinewoods.

Everywhere the past and present come together, linked by the Church to exist harmoniously side by side. The orthodox calendar is faithfully observed and rituals reaching back many centuries still play an important role in the lives of the people. This is particularly so on the islands and in the rural areas of mainland Greece. Sunday mornings hear the clamour of church bells, with little regard for Saturday's late night revellers.

In this book I have tried to gather together the different threads of Greek history and weave them into the fabric of today to span 3,000 years of history (in an interesting way). It is impossible to cover such events as the Persian wars, the Peloponnese wars and the whole Byzantine period in detail. My aim has been to chronicle the past through the Greek people and, at the same time, to include enough information to give readers a desire to know more about Greece and its magnificent history.

ONE

A brief history of Greece

The Dark Age

Greece has fired the imagination of the western world for centuries.
Like others before them, the Romans were deeply impressed by its
magnificence, yet did not refrain from sacking its cities, removing
its treasures and incorporating it into their empire. It was
fashionable for young Romans to study at the university of Athens
— Greek was the vogue. But this was later. We still start our
historical journey at the period known as the Dark Age, about 1200
BC. This lasted for about 450 years.

The Dorians, a warlike people from northern Greece, attacked
the Mycenaean cities already weakened by internal strife. The
Mycenaeans were an enterprising and accomplished people but,
unlike the peace-loving Minoans of Crete, enjoyed such pastimes as
war, brigandry and piracy! They had many military adventures on
the coast of Asia Minor, including the seige of the city of Troy
which is said to have lasted for 10 years. Agamemnon came from
Mycenae and led the ancient Greeks into the Trojan war.

The people of Mycenae originally came from Crete around the
year 1600 BC bringing with them all the skills and cultural
refinements of the great Minoan civilisation. The palaces they built
were surrounded by fortifications, with walls ten feet thick.
Incredibly rich, they placed in their tombs gold and silver artistically
wrought into deathmasks, breastplates, drinking cups and jewellery;
they even used fine sheets of gold to wrap around the bodies of their
royal family.

They were advanced in medical skills, as one skeleton proves: the
fractured skull had been neatly trepanned. This is the earliest record
of this type of surgery in Europe. Records have been found by
archaeologists of an efficient and highly developed bureaucracy;
taxes, agricultural stores, slaves, horses and chariots — and even

spare parts for chariots — were all recorded. One record stated that 'one pair of wheels bound with bronze and one pair of wheels bound with silver — unfit for service'.

Around 1200 BC this vital and brilliant civilisation came to an abrupt end. The conquering Dorians lived in the burnt-out Mycenaean palaces, but did not rebuild them. Art and records ceased; the Dark Age had begun. The meticulous Mycenaean society was plunged into total disarray by the Dorian assault. Many people fled and became dispossessed, purposeless wanderers. The Dorians moved south seizing the Laconian plain. Pressing further south, they sailed across the Mediterranean to Crete, conquering and subjugating it completely. From Crete they moved on to Rhodes and the neighbouring islands. Apart from a few pockets of Mycenaean culture, most of the Archaen, or ancient world, fell apart. The old stability and order was gone.

Lion Gate, Mycenae: entrance to the acropolis. The massive lintel is 15ft long and 6½ ft thick.

The Treasury of Atrius or Tomb of Agamemnon, the most impressive of the nine tholos tombs which resemble huge beehives. Constructed about 1300 BC, it ties in well with the accepted date of the Trojan War, about 1100 BC.

In the first centuries after the fall of the Mycenaean civilisation, each city became a separate unit, governed by a military style commander and his captains. Military rulers became kings and ruled by divine right.

The king became the religious leader of the city as well as its secular head. Slowly, like a growing flower, urban life evolved again. New cultural patterns emerged, crossing the local boundaries. People mingled and shared ideas and skills. The Greeks' own name for themselves, Hellenes, originated in the Dark Age. Greek pottery took on a distinctive Hellenic look, and a common language developed with regional dialects. From these rather tentative beginnings, the Hellenic civilisation eventually came into being, bringing with it a sense of cultural unity.

Athens had been able to repel the Dorian onslaught, and many Mycenaeans found a safe refuge there. The Acropolis was a natural fortress. Sparta on the other hand, was settled by the Dorians.

centuries later, Athens and Sparta would represent opposing philosophies — the former representing intellectual and political freedom, and the latter, hard military discipline.

Sparta was organised as a military camp, and kept this character until all the neighbouring settlements in the Laconian plain were subdued. Surprisingly, for a time, Sparta became one of the brightest centres of the culture that flowered at the close of the Dark Age.

Sparta produced exquisite pottery and was famous for its festivals of song and dance, but as soon as military concerns became paramount, these activities faded and life, to coin a phrase, became 'spartan' once more. Life was rigidly controlled from birth to death and family life became practically non-existent. Everyone belonged to the State. By sharp contrast, the citizens of Athens were able to move freely. Greeks sailed out into the Aegean to find new homes among the islands on the western coast of Asia Minor. The emigré colonies of Greeks in and around the Aegean came to be called Ionia, the first colony being Naxos, followed by Chios and Samos. The new settlers were not always welcomed by the native population as they protected themselves in walled towns. In time, these precautions stood the colonists in good stead, for as their colonies prospered, they were harassed by the Cimmerians and Lydians who had, one after the other, supplanted the Hittites in Asia Minor. The settlers did not recreate the old Mycenaean world, but they had at least built a new one.

It was during the close of the Dark Age in the eighth century BC that the first alphabet emerged. This made a dramatic change in the lives of the people.

Greek resistance to the Persian empire

Whilst Greek culture gathered strength and assurance, the Persians, to the east, were also expanding under their powerful ruler King Cyrus the Great. He had already combined Persia, Media and Assyria into one vast empire, so it was only a matter of time before he conquered all the major Ionian colonies — all except the island of Samos. Polycrates, the tyrannical leader of the island, was a determined soldier as well as a lavish patron of the arts. He was also a pioneer in engineering, commissioning a breakwater for his harbour and a tunnel to be dug through a mountain for his water supply. But even Polycrates was no match for the invading Persians. They managed to lure him to the Asian mainland where in 520 BC they captured and crucified him. Persia was now master of all Ionia.

The Greeks on the mainland did little to help their fellow countrymen, the exception being Sparta which sent an envoy to the Persians to protest against their actions and remind them that Sparta claimed the right to protect all Greek cities — but their protest fell on deaf ears. For a while the Ionians reluctantly submitted to their new masters but, Greek nature being what it is, they rebelled in 499 BC. They received some help from Athens, but it was not enough, and the Ionians were eventually overwhelmed by the Persians, who burned and sacked Miletus as retribution, transplanting part of its population to the Persian gulf, more than a thousand miles away. It was a bitter blow for the Greeks. Miletus had been the richest and most brilliant of the Ionian cities. Later, when the Athenian poet Phrynichus turned its story into a tragedy, *The Capture of Miletus,* his Athenian audience was so distraught that the playwright was fined 1,000 drachmas for depressing them!

Darius I, who had succeeded to the Persian throne after King Cyrus, was the sole ruler of an empire extending from Egypt to India, and from the Persian gulf to the Black Sea, an incredible two million square miles. He was a shrewd and aggressive leader, astute financially and interested in the economic advantages of applied engineering. He built a canal between the Nile and the Red Sea, and a network of roads for the deployment of his vast armies. One of these roads ran 1500 miles from Susa near the Persian gulf to Sardis near the Aegean. Herodotus, the Greek historian who wrote an excellent account of the Persian wars, said of him, 'Darius looked to making a gain in everything.'

In 492 BC Darius made his first attack against the Greek mainland in the north at Thrace and Macedonia, with the intention of moving south. The first part of the invasion was successful, but having wrecked his ships rounding Mount Athos in Macedonia he was forced to return home. Darius sent messages to all the Greek states demanding their submission. Some states complied, but not Athens and Sparta.

Darius attacked again. He sent a fleet of 600 ships and a large efficient army; their destination was Marathon. Darius's intention was to march overland to Athens. With the enemy on their doorstep, the Athenians finally woke up to the danger, and in an incredibly short time decided on a strategy that turned out to be flawless. Miltiades, a brilliant general, persuaded his fellow generals not to wait for the Persian onslaught, but to take the offensive and march immediately to Marathon. This not only astounded the invaders, but also saved the countryside from devastation. The

Persians were beaten back into the sea. Herodotus claimed that Marathon cost the Persians 6400 men against the Athenians' 192. Miltiades despatched the runner Phidipides to Athens, a distance of 22 miles, with the news of their victory. Gasping out his message: 'We have been victorious,' he fell down dead.

The Athenians who died at Marathon were buried in a great commemorative mound which still stands on the site of the battle, and the survivors were held in high honour all their lives. It was a battle that has never faded from history and, like the story of the lone Marathon runner, never will. Apart from petty quarrels between the states, the Greeks lived in relative peace for the next ten years.

The death of Darius and the succession of his son Xerxes in 485 BC did not change the plans of the Persians. Marathon was a constant thorn in their flesh and Xerxes was a determined man. As the Persian threat loomed once more on the Greek horizon, Sparta took the initiative and invited all the Greek states to meet with a view to ending their feuds and combining their forces to defend themselves against their common enemy. They called themselves the **League of the Greeks** and Sparta was given command of all their forces. The war with Persia was to rage for over 35 years, ending in an astonishing Greek victory against the might of the Persian army.

Apart from the professional war-machine of the Spartans, most of the Greek forces were made up of ordinary citizens. Also the League never completely agreed on a common strategy. Each state put its own interests first, and yet with the odds against them, they emerged victorious, a success which filled the Greeks with justifiable pride and patriotism. The victory also left Sparta the most important power in Greece. The Spartan forces had fought well and were held in high esteem by the other Greek states, but Athens remained the jewel in the Greek crown and flourished with a phenomenal vitality. This was the Athenian Golden Age, without parallel in the history of the world.

The Athenian League

The citizens of Athens, having discovered the meaning of liberty and
democracy, saw it as their duty to impart their knowledge to others. The Persian defeat gave them an excellent opportunity. Although Sparta gained enormous prestige for its war effort, quarrelling broke out between its aristocrats and kings for political leadership, thus weakening its stability. Sparta reverted to an isolated state

Pella, capital of the Macedonians and birthplace of Alexander the Great

devoting all its energies to maintaining its own boundaries in the Peloponnese. This left Athens free to take over the leadership of Greece. It proposed the formation of a league of Greek states and, during the winter of 478 – 477 BC, this was set up. The League numbered 250 – 300 members and each state contributed according to its resources.

Athens, with the support of the League, soon renewed the Persian offensive, and in 468 BC destroyed a new Persian fleet as it lay at anchor awaiting Xerxes's order for another invasion of the Aegean. This important victory justified the League's existence and strengthened the loose knots that bound it together.

The transition from the League as a confederacy to an empire ruled by Athens was a logical progression of events. Greece was now divided into two camps, Sparta and Athens. The Spartan alliance comprised most of the Peloponnese, the Isthmus of Corinth and Megara. The Athenian empire held the Aegean islands and the coast of Asia Minor. With two powerful camps politically opposed to each other, it is little wonder that war became inevitable. The Peloponnesian war began in 431 BC and lasted continuously for more than 25 years. It was a bitter demoralising war as Greek fought Greek. For Athens, defeat was total. Its lands were devastated and the war reached the very walls of the city. Yet during this turbulent time Athens never neglected the arts and raised two of the loveliest temples on the Acropolis, the little temple to Athena Nike and the Erechtheum. Faced with starvation Athens surrendered and pledged its allegiance to Sparta. By the terms of the peace treaty all its foreign possessions were lost and its fleet forfeited.

Athens had to recover from the ravages of war, but its political problems stemmed mainly from Sparta's attempts to install a government compatible with its own interests and policies, the outcome of which was the appointment of a Council of 30 men, later known as the **Thirty Tyrants.** Instead of governing the city they spent their time persecuting opponents and confiscating property. Many men were put to death without regard for the law. In less than a year the Athenians drove the Thirty from the city. Spartan policies failed elsewhere and a golden opportunity to unite Greece was lost. In Athens, with the tyrants gone, a measure of democracy was restored; the city began to heal its war wounds and a new era of brilliance emerged.

The Rising power of Macedonia

On its northern frontier, Greece's somewhat ambiguous relative, Macedonia, was lifting an interested eye towards its cousin in the south. The Macedonian kings were of Greek descent and aspired to be Greeks, although they had fought against the Greeks in the Persian wars. In 359 BC, Philip II succeeded to the throne of Macedonia with a determination to make himself master of all Greek lands. He began by controlling the outer regions of Macedonia, then moved south into Thessaly and east into Thrace. He was a brilliant commander and headed a professional army trained in the new ideas of warfare. His skill in diplomacy matched his military genius. Instead of annexing a state by war he preferred to secure it by marriage. In all he had six or seven wives!

Philip marched south and was preparing to take Delphi, whose sacred shrine of Apollo made it the centre of Greek religious life. The Greeks looked towards Athens for leadership, but Athens was divided. One side was led by Isocrates, who believed the Persians were still their greatest threat, and the other by Demosthenes, the greatest of all Greek orators. He believed in liberty and urged the Athenians to be prepared to fight for it. Through his brilliant oratory and eloquent arguments he managed to persuade his fellow countrymen to oppose Philip.

Thebes joined Athens in the ensuing war, but in the summer of 338 BC it was all over. A victorious Philip called a congress of all the Greek states at Corinth, and brought most of them under his military leadership in the **League of Corinth.** Philip above all others realised that unity for Greece was vital and, excepting Sparta, he succeeded in this.

In 336 BC Philip's eyes turned towards the Persian empire, but just as he was about to start his offensive he was murdered at the marriage feast of his daughter. His son Alexander, at the age of 20, succeeded to his father's throne.

Philip's policy of expansion was firmly established and the young Alexander had only to pick up where his father had left off. Unlike Philip, whose caution and diplomacy had served him well, Alexander preferred to move swiftly. The sheer force of his vitality overcame the risks he took. In courage, endurance, strength and confidence he excelled, and he was no less endowed in his strength of affections, loyalties and generosity. Alexander's boyhood teacher, Aristotle, taught his young pupil a love for art and poetry, and gave him a lasting interest in philosophy and science.

6   One of Alexander's chief objectives was to continue his father's

The Arch of Galerius, Salonika, was built by the emperor to commemorate his victories over the Persians in 297 AD.

plan and invade Persia. For centuries Persia had continued to interfere in Greek affairs and constantly oppressed the Greek colonies of Asia Minor. Alexander also wanted desperately to be identified with Greece, and the best way to do this was to attack Greece's ancient enemy. In 334 BC he crossed the Hellespont and quickly defeated the Persian forces gathered on the Asian side. He sent back 300 suits of Persian armour to Athens with a message: 'Alexander, son of Philip and the Greeks, except the Spartans, has won this spoil from the barbarians of Asia.'

Alexander's plan was to destroy the Persian army, but it was not long before he decided to take the Persian empire. This he did without losing a single battle. After his conquest of the Persian empire, Alexander turned south and headed into India. He crossed the Hindu Kush mountains, followed the river Kabul down to the river Indus, and crossed overland to the river Hydaspes. Here he fought one of the most difficult battles of his career with the Indian king, Porus, whose army outnumbered his. But Alexander was much more experienced in warfare and outwitted Porus. It was here that his much loved horse Bucephalus was killed. He founded a city on the site of the battle and named it Bucephala.

Alexander continued to march south through India, but his men were becoming restless. Taking the Persian empire was one thing, but the invasion of India was another. They were tired of war and they longed for home. The army refused to go on. Alexander waited three days for them to change their minds. Realising their determination, he gave orders for their return. He divided his army into three, sending one home by sea, another following a northerly route, and the third under his command, returning through the southern regions. Much of Alexander's route was through burning desert. The heat was so intense that they had to march by night. Food was short and the pack animals had to be slaughtered. By the spring of 323 BC, he reached Babylon and immediately began to regroup his army for an invasion of Arabia. But in early June he was struck down with fever and on 13 June 323 BC he died; he was 33 years old. The legend of Alexander the Great was born.

Defeat by Rome

In the 300 years that followed Alexander's death a new era evolved, the Hellenistic age. The political structure of Alexander's great empire disintegrated almost immediately. India reverted to its old rulers and Alexander's generals, eager for power, divided what was left. In Greece the League of Corinth fell apart, and once more the country was divided into two camps, the **Aetolian** and the **Achaen Leagues.** But Alexander's influence still remained in Asia.

Greece maintained its independence until covetous eyes fell upon the nation once more. By 146 BC, Rome had overrun the whole of Greece, and it became a small province of the vast Roman empire. Rome learnt much from Greece. Many works of art were plundered and found their way into the villas of eminent Romans. Greek tutors were employed for the education of Roman children. The cultural tradition of Greece exercised a definite influence on the great Roman civilisation which, through its network of government, found its way to the entire western world.

The Roman empire stretched from northern England through France, Spain, North Africa, Egypt, Italy, Greece and Turkey to Syria and grew too large for effective government. Unrest within Rome itself reverberated throughout the empire. About 286 AD, it was decided to set up four regional governments in an attempt to stop the rot. The emperor, Diocletian, set up court at Nicomedia in what is now northern Turkey. His three co-rulers were Maxentius, ruling Italy and Africa from Milan; Constantius, ruling France, Britain and Spain from Trier in modern Germany; and Galerius, ruling Illyria, Macedonia and Greece from Salonica.

The division of the empire solved nothing and civil war soon broke out. On the death of Constantius, Constantine succeeded his father. It was while he was encamped with his army outside the walls of Rome, waiting to attack, that he had a vision. A gold cross was silhouetted against the sun's rays and had purple streamers flowing from it. The initials of Christ were clearly visible and some accounts also mention the words *hoc signo vince* meaning 'by this sign win your victory'. The fact that the royal colour of purple was seen suggested that the message was intended for Constantine. He immediately ordered the Christian monogram to be displayed on his soldiers' standards and won the battle for Rome.

When Constantine became the sole ruler of the whole Roman empire he decided to move his capital to Byzantium in the eastern province. Byzantium was founded by Byzas in 675 BC. Byzas and his followers were Greek and had come from Megara in Attica. Before their departure they had consulted the Oracle for advice as to where they should found their new colony. The advice they received was confused: 'Go and settle opposite the city of the blind' it had said. The settlers finally reached the south-eastern extremity of Thrace near the Bosphorus. There they found a triangle of land projecting into the sea: it was strategically perfect. The promontory

Delphi, home of the oracle, spectacularly sited on the slopes of Parnassos.

was overlooking the Greek settlement of Chalcedon across the Bosphorus. Byzas and his followers decided that the people of Chalcedon must have been blind indeed not to choose this site for their own colony.

Constantine soon realised that Byzantium, although strategically perfect to cope with the ever-present threat from the east, was too small to serve as the capital of his empire. In 324 AD he set his men to work, constructing administrative buildings, a palace, forum and a great church, dedicated to *Aghia Sophia,* the Holy Wisdom. His new capital, Constantinople, was completed in only six years.

Constantine was the first emperor to legalise Christianity. When his mother, Helen, set out on a pilgrimage to the holy land he asked her to bring back a piece of the true cross. This she did and the fragment became the most venerated relic in Byzantium. Although Constantine steered the course towards Christianity, he remained a pagan until he asked, on his death bed, to be received into the Christian church. It was in the reign of Theodosius I in 381 AD that Christianity became the official religion of the empire. Constantinople was to remain the centre for Christian thought for a thousand years. Constantine's capital was ruled by Romans although the inhabitants were mostly Greek, and Latin remained the official language until the fifth century.

In 385 AD on the death of Theodosius I, it was decided to divide the empire into two parts. The eastern empire was ruled from Constantinople by the new emperor, Arcadius, and the subordinate western empire governed from Ravenna. Greece became part of the eastern empire and an integral part of the Byzantine world, exercising a great influence on art and culture. By 476 AD Rome had fallen to the Goths, and the last of the Imperial house, Romulus Augustus, was deposed. The emperor of Byzantium at that time was Zeno, and such was his prestige that the German chieftain Theodoric, although victorious, felt it necessary that Zeno should recognise him officially as *Patricius* of Rome and prefect of Italy. The ties were very strong between Rome and Byzantium, so much so that Byzantine culture was adopted by Theodoric.

The aim of all the emperors was to make Constantinople the cultural as well as the political centre of the known world. After the closure of Athens university by Justinian in 529, and later the loss of the universities of Antioch, Alexandria and Beirut to the Muslims, the university of Constantinople was the only one available to the Christian world. By 856 it had become so overcrowded that a second university was founded. In 1405 a third university was established solely for the training of civil servants and

*Mistras, Peloponnese, last stronghold of the Byzantines after the
fall of Constantinople. The city is built into the hillside with
spectacular views across the plain of Sparta.*

lawyers, a good indication of the highly developed administrative
and commercial skills of the city.

In Byzantium, Greeks and Romans lived side by side merging into
a united Christian culture and way of life. Although pagan, the
Greek myths were well known to the Byzantines whose love of
symbolism expressed itself in literature and art. Icons became a
physical expression of Christian belief and are an important feature
of the Orthodox Church. The Byzantines were also prolific church
builders and many of their churches are still in use today.

Throughout its 1000 years, Byzantium was not a dictatorial state;
its people were free, but war was ever present. Slowly the empire
shrunk, losing first Spain then Italy. In 613 Jerusalem fell to the
Persians who then marched on Constantinople but were
miraculously repelled. The rise of Islam and the ambitions of
Byzantium's Slavic neighbours, as well as the occupation by Franks
and Venetians and the attack of other Christian Crusaders, all took
their toll on its vitality. In 1453 the Ottoman Turks attacked
Constantinople. Their ruthless armies devastated and plundered
Constantine's beautiful city and the rest of Greece. Constantine XI

23

was the last emperor of Byzantium and died fighting gallantly for his capital.

The modern Greek state

Greece endured 400 years of brutal oppression until the War of Independence of 1821. Provoked by Turkish brutality and inspired by an intense desire for liberty, the Greeks rebelled and finally gained their freedom. In 1832 Greece was declared an independent kingdom and the National Assembly at Nauphlia ratified the election of Prince Otho of Bavaria as king of Greece. He arrived at Nauphlia, the capital of his new kingdom, in 1833. In 1834 the capital was transferred to Athens.

Rebellion broke out in 1862, and a provisional government was set up, led by the politician Voulgaris who declared an end to King Otho's reign. Few Greeks regretted his departure.

In 1863, the son of the king of Denmark was proclaimed the first king of the Hellenes. King George I was only 18 years old when he came to the throne and he was still in power at the outbreak of the first and second Balkan wars in 1912 and 1913 respectively.

However, he was murdered in March 1913 in Salonica and his son, Constantine, became king. In 1916 a provisional government was set up in Salonica by Venizelos, the deposed Prime Minister, and the country was now divided. In 1917, King Constantine I abdicated in favour of his second son Alexander, who died in 1920; Constantine was then recalled to the throne.

In 1919-1922 the Graeco-Turkish campaign in Asia Minor saw the expulsion of the Greek population and the end of a long history of Hellenism in Asia Minor. The Armistice agreement was signed on 11 October 1922. A peace conference was assembled at Lausanne on 21 November 1922 but the difficult negotiations delayed the final signing of the **Treaty of Lausanne** until 14 July 1923. There were over one million Greek refugees from Asia Minor, a catastrophe of unparalleled proportions in Greek history.

At this time of national crises a 'revolutionary' committee of army officers assumed power. King Constantine I was handed an ultimatum on 26 September 1922 and consequently left the country and the throne, which then passed to his son George.

In 1924 King George II was asked to leave Greece until the future of the monarchy was decided. In March 1924 a republic was etablished, but in 1935 King George II returned to his throne. After the outbreak of the Second World War, the Italians invaded Greece

The monastery of Varlaam, founded in 1517. The high precipitous rocks of Meteora were home for 24 monasteries and a host of hermitages over the centuries, out of which only six now remain.

and between 1944 and 1949 there were two communist rebellions.

King George II died in 1947 and his brother Paul succeeded to the throne and reigned until his death in 1964. His son Constantine ascended the throne, but in 1967 the democratic government was overthrown and King Constantine II left Greece. The military dictatorship fell in 1974 and parliamentary democracy was restored.

TWO

The Olympian Gods

The ancient Greeks believed that in the beginning of the world there
was a great void which they called Chaos and out of which Mother
Earth emerged, who bore a son called Uranus. Uranus fathered the
elder gods or Titans and among them was the terrible Cronus.
Mother Earth persuaded the Titans to attack Uranus in revenge for
his imprisonment of the Cyclopes, the one-eyed giants. Cronus crept
up to Uranus as he lay sleeping and, taking a flint sickle provided
by Mother Earth, castrated him. Cronus then released the Cyclopes
who gave him sovereignty over all the earth. As soon as he was sole
ruler, Cronus imprisoned the Cyclopes again and married his sister
Rhea.

It was prophesied by Mother Earth and his father Uranus, as he
lay dying, that one of Cronus's sons would dethrone him. To avoid
this eventuality, Cronus swallowed the children that Rhea bore him.
Zeus was spared this fate and deposing his father, led the next
deities, the Olympians, whom the Greeks worshipped throughout
the Golden Age of their history.

It is interesting to note that Cronus, whose name means Time,
was later portrayed by the Romans as old Father Time, a benevolent
old man holding a sickle and hour-glass!

Zeus
Ruler of mount Olympus, king of gods and man, god of the
weather, sixth child of Cronus and his wife Rhea, was to have been
devoured by his father like his brothers and sisters; but his mother
hid him and gave Cronus a stone. When Zeus grew up he gave
Cronus an emetic so that he spewed up his sons and daughters. They
then conspired with Zeus against the elder gods. Using lightning
stolen from the Titans, the rebel children won the battle for the
universe.

Pallas Athena

The virgin patron of arts and crafts, goddess of wisdom and protectress in war of those who worshipped her, sprang full grown and fully armed from the head of Zeus. In the beginning Athena was depicted as a young girl, but as Athens — named after her — aged, so did the goddess. Later she was shown as a more motherly figure protecting all those who worshipped her. She valued intellect and the gentle arts of living. She was reputed to have invented the flute. She helped the Greeks to win Troy and established the rule of law and the concept of mercy. Her gift of the olive tree to mankind won her the devotion of Athens.

Apollo, from the temple of Zeus, Olympia, his right arm outstretched in an imperious gesture as he watches, determined that victory be awarded to the righteous.

27

Apollo

Son of Zeus, he was associated with the basic Greek precepts 'Know thyself' and 'Nothing in excess'. He seized the oracle at Delphi from Python, a priestess who gave advice to Greece, some good and some bad. Apollo was god of the sun and patron of music, poetry, philosophy, astronomy, mathematics, medicine and science.

Artemis

Virgin goddess of the moon, and twin sister of Apollo, she was the guardian of cities, animal life and women. Women prayed to her for easy childbirth.

Aphrodite

She was the goddess of love and beauty and wife of Hephaestus. Wherever she walked flowers sprang up and doves flew about her. She bore her lover Ares several children and among them were Fear and Terror. Wearing her magic girdle, she had the power to seduce even the wisest gods and often tempted Zeus, her adopted father.

Hera

Protectress of marriage, married women, children and the home, she was both wife and sister to Zeus. It is said that Zeus courted her for 300 years before she consented to marry him. Hera appears in the stories of the gods as a betrayed wife, torturing the young women whom Zeus loved.

Demeter

Goddess of crops and giver of grain and fruit, she gave the world the gift of the plough.

Hermes

Zeus's son and the messenger of the gods to men, he was the protector of sheep and cattle, of mischief-makers and the guardian of travellers. When he was born, he stole Apollo's cattle and in the ensuing pursuit laid a false trail. When caught by Silenus and his satyrs, the nymph Cyllene protested that he was too young to steal! He was the god not only of commerce and the market-place, but also of orators and writers.

Poseidon

God of the sea and earthquakes and giver of horses to man, Poseidon built himself a palace of gold deep in the Aegean sea. The Greeks were grateful for the horse but wary of the treacherous seas, so they prayed to Poseidon for a safe sea voyage

Poseidon, god of the sea.

Dionysus
The god of the vine and fertility, of a happy life and hospitality, was one of the later members of the Olympian family. He was the son of Zeus by a mortal mother, Semele. He was driven mad by Hera's jealousy and wandered the earth accompanied by satyrs and maenads. A symbol of revelry, he gave Greece the gift of wine.

Ares
God of war, symbolised by the vulture, Ares was hated by Zeus and Hera, his father and mother. Hades liked him, for his wars increased the population of the underworld! He was held in awe by the Greeks but was never the object of adoration. His love affair

The Hermes of Praxiteles the Sculptor (fourth century BC) was excavated at Olympia in 1877. The ancient traveller Pausanias, in the second century AD, described it as a 'stone Hermes carrying the infant Dionysios'. It was found in the temple of Hera, exactly where Pausanias had seen it.

with Aphrodite caused many problems amongst the Olympian family.

Hephaestus

The God of fire, artists, and blacksmiths was expelled from Olympus by his own mother, Hera, because of his lameness. Many creations came from his forges, among them Pandora, the first mortal woman, into whom the gods breathed life. Husband of Aphrodite he built himself a magnificent palace on Olympus and had mechanical servants. He was held in high esteem.

THREE

Heroes and great men

Heroes of Greek mythology

In Greek mythology the heroes, as distinguished from the gods, were mortal, or rather super-mortal, but some did claim descent from the gods. Their feats were sung by poets and depicted in works of art that expressed a purely Greek character. Even today authors, artists and composers still find inspiration in the stories of these heroes.

Io

She was loved by Zeus who turned her into a heifer to hide her from his wife, Hera. Hera was not deceived and put the heifer under the guard of Argus, a man with a hundred eyes. She escaped and Zeus restored her to human form. They had a son who started the line of Heracles.

Deucalion and Pyrrha

Deucalion and his wife were the sole survivors of the great flood which Zeus used to destroy a world that had grown wicked. The couple floated on the waters in a large boat which they had stocked with provisions. As the waters receded, the couple gave thanks for their deliverance and heard a voice telling them to throw the bones of their mother behind them. At first they refused, but then realised that the earth was their mother and her bones were stones. The stones they threw turned into human beings who re-populated the world.

Heracles

He was the son of Zeus by a mortal mother, and is best remembered for his labours, done at the bidding of King Eurystheus of Mycenae. These were:

1. Choked the 'invulnerable' lion of Nemea to death.
2. Killed the nine-headed Hydra.
3. Captured a golden-horned stag after chasing it for a year.
4. Trapped a great boar by running it to exhaustion.
5. Diverted two rivers to flush out the foul Augean stables.
6. Drove away the voracious Stymphalian birds and, as they flew up, shot them down with his bow and arrows.
7. Captured the savage bull of Minos.
8. Ensnared the man-eating mares of Diomedes.
9. Asked for and obtained the girdle of Hippolyta, Queen of the Amazons.
10. Stole the cattle of Geryon, a three-bodied monster and, in the process, set up the Pillars of Heracles. (Now Gibraltar and Ceuta.)
11. Held up the sky whilst he sent Atlas to find the golden apples of the Hesperides, then tricked Atlas into resuming the burden of the heavens.
12. Captured Cerberus, the three-headed dog of Hades.

Oedipus

While journeying to Thebes, Oedipus killed an old man in a quarrel. He successfully challenged the Sphinx, a monster which devoured those who could not solve this riddle: 'What creature goes on four feet in the morning, two at noonday, and three in the evening?' Oedipus's answer was: 'Man, who first crawls, then walks and finally must use a stick.' He was rewarded with the hand of Jocasta, the widowed Queen of Thebes. It had been prophesied that Oedipus would murder his father and marry his mother, and the prophecy had now come true, for Jocasta was his mother, and the man he had
killed was her husband and his father. When Jocasta and Oedipus discovered their terrible sin, she killed herself and he put his eyes out and wandered throughout Greece. Athens finally gave him shelter, and when he died he promised that his body would save the city from harm.

Perseus

As a child he was cast into the sea by his grandfather Agrisius king of Tiryns, who was trying to forestall a prophesy that one day the child would kill him. Perseus was rescued and when he grew up went to the land of the Gorgons. These creatures were so ugly that whoever looked upon them was turned to stone. They had wings, body scales and their hair was made of twisting serpents. With the help of the gods, Perseus killed Medusa, one of the Gorgons, and

ΠΕΡΙΚΛΗΣ
ΞΑΝΘΙΠΠΟΥ
ΑΘΗΝΑΙΟΣ

34

carried her head away. He freed Andromeda, a princess threatened by a man-eating sea serpent and married her. By using Medusa's head, he turned his mother Danae's insistent suitor to stone, and fulfilled the prophecy by accidentally killing his grandfather.

Cadmus

He was commanded by Apollo to create the city of Thebes. First of all, he had to slay the guardian of the site, a dragon which killed all his companions. Instructed by Athena, he planted the dragon's teeth which gave forth armed men. They fought each other until only five remained; together with the five Cadmus founded Thebes.

Europa

Sister of Cadmus, she was gathering flowers when Zeus appeared to her in the form of a white and beautiful bull with a silver circle on his brow, and horns like the moon's crescent. Europa, impressed by his beauty, was persuaded to mount the bull. She crossed the sea on his back, became his bride and bore him three sons. Eventually she gave her name to the continent of Europe.

Jason

With his band of heroes, among them Heracles, Orpheus, Castor and Pollux, he sailed in the ship *Argo* in search of the Golden Fleece. They had many adventures, fighting Harpies and skilfully avoiding battle with Amazons. The heroes, called the Argonauts, reached Colchis on the Black Sea where Jason seized the Golden Fleece and fled, accompanied by the witch-maiden Medea, daughter of the king of Colchis. Jason and Medea lived happily together until Jason left her to marry Creusa. Medea murdered Creusa, then killed her own children and took flight in a chariot drawn by dragons. Jason was distraught and wandered throughout the land. One day he lay down in the shade of *Argo;* the rotted prow suddenly fell and killed him.

Theseus

Relative of Heracles and his rival for heroic honours, Theseus cleared the roads leading into Athens of bandits. He sailed to Crete to kill the half-man half-bull Minotaur. As King of Athens he

(opposite) *Pericles dominated the Athenian Golden Age, using his social position to win popular support. The satirists nicknamed him 'Onion Head', a feature he tried to conceal beneath a helmet whenever possible.*

brought peace and order to the country. Ultimately he united Attica into a single state. He sailed with Jason on the *Argo* in search of the Golden Fleece, took part with other Argonauts in the Calydonian hunt for a terrible boar and fought the Centaurs.

Atlanta
The most adventurous of women, Atlanta took part in the heroes' hunt for the Calydonian boar. She offered to marry any of her suitors who could beat her in a foot race. Those who were losers would forfeit their lives. Daring Melanion won her hand by carrying three golden apples into the race. Whenever Atlanta took the lead, he threw a golden apple in front of her; as she stopped to pick them up, he passed her and so won the race.

Bellerophon
Son of Glaucus and grandson of Sisyphus, he was ordered by the King of Lycia to kill the Chimaera, a fire-breathing monster which had the head of a lion, the body of a goat, and a snake for a tail. Mounted on Pegasus, the winged horse, Bellerophon soared above the Chimaera. Weakening it with arrows, he finally killed it by pouring molten lead down its throat. Later Bellerophon angered the gods by daring to fly on Pegasus to join them on mount Olympus. When the horse threw him, he was left to wander the earth, crippled and blind and despised by the deities.

The heroes of Troy
Achilles was the most famous warrior on the Greek side in the Trojan war, well-known for his bravery and courage. The only part of his body that was mortal was his heel where, as a child, his mother held him in the sacred river to give him immortality.

Hector was the greatest of the Trojan warriors. He was slain by Achilles, who allowed him honourable burial.

Ajax, in valour and beauty second only to Achilles among the Greeks, after realising that he had behaved ignobly towards his friends, ended his life in suicide.

Agamemnon was the commander of the Greeks and brother-in-law of **Helen** whose kidnap by the Trojans started the war. Agamemnon was murdered by his wife, **Clytaemnestra,** in revenge for having sacrificed the life of their daughter to Artemis to ensure fair winds for the sea passage to Troy.

Odysseus, King of Ithaca, famed for his shrewdness, created the ruse of the Trojan Horse which finally won victory for the Greeks at Troy.

Great men of Greece

Sophocles 496-406 BC

Born at Colonus just outside Athens, he was the greatest playwright of classical Greece. Wealthy, handsome and brilliant, he earned the love and respect of all his contemporaries. He was a friend of Pericles and, though not a politician, held several public offices, both civil and military. He was also a close friend of Herodotus, the poet and historian, and was leader of a literary circle; He spent all his 90 years in Athens and preferred the company of his friends to the patronage of kings.

During his lifetime Sophocles witnessed the long struggle against Persian aggression and the soul-destroying Peloponnesian war. He was a prolific writer throughout his long life and wrote one of his greatest plays, *Oedipus at Colonus,* just one year before his death. Of the more than 100 plays he wrote only seven have survived intact.

Here are some quotations from Sophocles. The first, in praise of the Athenian countryside, is taken from *Oedipus at Colonus.*

> 'With the heavenly dew of morn,
> The golden crocus and narcissus grow
> To adorn the crowns of the ancient gods.
> The sleepless springs are never dry,
> Feeding the pure water of Kephesos;
> Ceaselessly rippling, meanders by,
> Creating life in the fertile earth,
> Filling with ripeness abundant birth.'

> 'There are many wonderful things, and nothing is more wonderful than man.'

> 'Not to be born is, past all prizing, best.'

Pericles 495-429 BC

He was a statesman, orator and general, and brought Athens to the peak of its power in Greece's Golden Age. Through democratic reforms and public works, he transformed the life of the city's 150,000 inhabitants.

Pericles's political genius and brilliant leadership kept him in power for 30 years. It was during his lifetime that the Acropolis was reconstructed with its temples: the Parthenon, Erechtheum, Propylaea and the temple of Athena Nike — a legacy that has lasted for 2,500 years.

Socrates was the son of a sculptor and a midwife. It is not known whether he had a career but he did serve in the army as an infantryman. With his strong, thick-set body and strutting gait he was a cartoonist's dream.

When the Peloponnesian war began, Pericles made his funeral oration, from which three quotations follow:

> 'Our constitution is called democracy because power is in the hands, not of a minority, but of the whole people. When it is a matter of settling private disputes, everyone is equal before the law. When it is a question of placing one person before another in positions of public responsibility, what matters is not membership of a particular class, but the ability which the man possesses.'

> 'Our love of what is beautiful does not lead to extravagance, our love of things of the mind, does not make us soft.'

> 'Famous men have the whole earth as their memorial.'

Socrates 469 – 399 BC

The origins of this great philosopher and orator are obscure. It is generally believed he was not an aristocrat. Untidy and shabbily dressed, he walked barefoot with little thought for his own comfort. His great contribution to philosophy was his searching inquiry into questions of morality. The Socratic view is that a man's conscience is a superior guide to correct behaviour than are the demands of society. He was the first philosopher in Greece to explore this line of thought. His method of teaching was based on questioning his pupils in his search for the truth. He was totally opposed to the theories of power and political expediency which were accepted at the time. His lack of personal ambition made him refuse to take money for his teaching, and he lived his life on the simplest of lines.

Young people were eager for his company, and clustered round him in the Gymnasia and other meeting-places. It is unfortunate that none of Socrates's original work has survived and we have to depend on the records of his contemporaries.

Because of his ruthless attacks on safe, traditional attitudes, some Athenians thought his teaching extremely dangerous. In 399 BC he was officially accused of introducing strange gods and corrupting the young, and on these charges he was brought to trial. Socrates refused to recant his teaching and defended his actions in a speech that angered his accusers. The quotation is an extract from the defence speech of Socrates, from Plato's *The Last Days of Socrates* (Penguin Classics):

'Gentlemen, so far from pleading on my own behalf, as might be supposed, I am really pleading on yours, to save you from misusing the gift of God by condemning me. If you put me to death, you will not easily find anyone to take my place. It is literally true (even if it sounds rather comical) that God has specially appointed me to this city, as though it were a large thoroughbred horse which because of its great size is inclined to be lazy and needs the stimulation of some stinging fly. It seems to me that God has attached me to this city to perform the office of such a fly; and all day long I never cease to settle here, there, and everywhere, rousing, persuading, reproving every one of you. You will not easily find another like me, gentlemen, and if you take my advice you will spare my life. I suspect, however, that before long you will take Anytus' advice and finish me off with a single slap; and then you will go on sleeping till the end of your days, unless God in his care for you sends someone to take my place.'

This speech was considered arrogant and Socrates was condemned to death. After he had drunk hemlock (a considerate form of execution) he talked quietly to his friends. Plato recorded his words as he had done many times before. He said of his teacher 'He was the wisest and most just and best of men.' And so died one of Athens's greatest citizens.

Here are just a few of his recorded words:

'It is a fact, Simnias, that true philosophers make dying their profession...'

'The unexamined life is not worth living.'

'It is already time to depart, for me to die, for you to go on living; which of us takes the better course, is concealed from anyone but God.'

Plato 429-347 BC
This powerful philosopher and writer was greatly influenced by his teacher, Socrates. He came from a family that had long played a prominent part in Athenian politics.

Plato was 30 when his teacher died, and his death scarred his spirit and altered the course of his life. He left Athens and travelled abroad, notably in Sicily, and was political adviser to Dionysius II,

Aristotle, son of a physician and friend of the Macedonian royal family, became teacher to Alexander. He founded the library and museum in Athens, which Alexander helped to finance.

ruler of Syracuse. He returned to Athens in 385 BC where he founded a school called the *Academus,* later to be known as the Academy. He wrote over 20 philosophical dialogues and his literary activity extended over half a century.

Plato was interested in mathematics, especially geometry. He took his mathematical ideas from the Pythagoreans, followers of the sixth century philosopher, Pythagoras. He believed that the entire universe was constructed on numerical relationships.

Plato like his teacher Socrates, was deeply involved in the search for truth and sought a cure for the ills of society, not in politics, but in philosophy. He revised many of his ideas during the course of his long life. He taught at the Academy until his death in 347 BC.

The following quotations are used as examples of Plato's teaching:

> 'Knowledge that is acquired under compulsion has no hold on the mind.'

> 'Until wisdom and political leadership meet in the same man, cities will never cease from ill, nor the human race.'

Aristotle 384-322 BC

Aristotle was one of the greatest thinkers who ever lived. He came from Macedonia to study at Plato's Academy and created a philosophy as influential as that of his teacher, but totally opposed to it. He believed that all theory must follow demonstrable fact, and based his system on direct observation and strict logic. His ideas made him the founder of modern scientific method, and his approach to all knowledge was that of an experimental scientist. If Plato was basically a mathematician, Aristotle was a biologist. He studied the biological structure of living things and devised classification for many types of plants and animals. He enquired into human society and behaviour and even studied weather patterns.

Unlike Plato, he did not reject Athens's recent past, but analysed its political structure instead, understanding both its strength and its weaknesses. He was profoundly humane, a trait not easily seen in his scientific writings, but clearly recognisable in his *Ethics*. Aristotle laid down the principles which formed the basis for the study of science for centuries.

The following examples briefly illustrate his philosophy of life:

> 'Man is by nature a political animal.'

> 'Probable impossibilities are to be preferred to improbable possibilities.'

> 'It is necessary to be immortal as far as we can.'

Hippocrates 460-377 BC

Hippocrates, the father of medicine, was a physician and teacher of medicine from the Island of Cos. He was an early advocate of good

The Hippocratic Oath

I swear by Apollo Physician, by Asclepius, by Health, By Heal-all, and by all the gods and goddesses, making them witnesses, that I will carry out, according to my ability and judgement, this oath and this indenture:

To regard my teacher in this art as equal to my parents to make him partner in my livelihood, and when he is in need of money to share mine with him: to consider his offspring equal to my brothers; to teach them this art, if they require to learn it, without fee or indenture; and to impart precept, oral instruction, and all the other learning, to my sons, to the sons of my teacher, and to pupils who have signed the indenture and sworn obedience to the physicians' Law, but to none other.

I will use treatment to help the sick according to my ability and judgement, but I will never use it to injure or wrong them. I will not give poison to anyone though asked to do so, nor will I suggest such a plan. Similarly I will not give a pessary to a woman to cause abortion. But in purity and in holiness I will guard my life and my art.

I will not use the knife on sufferers from stone, but I will give place to such as are craftsmen therein. Into whatsoever houses I enter, I will do so to help the sick, keeping myself free from all intentional wrong-doing and harm, especially from fornication with woman or man, bond or free.

Whatsoever in the course of practice I see or hear (or even outside my practice in social intercourse) that ought never to be published abroad, I will not divulge, but consider such things to be holy secrets. Now if I keep this oath and break it not, may I enjoy honour, in my life and art, among all men for all time; but if I transgress and forswear myself, may the opposite befall me.

Hippocrates, born on Cos, belonged to the 'family of the Asklepiadae', (a group of doctors claiming descent from Asklepios, the great physician, who believed medicine was a rational science and that disease was not a punishment by the gods.)

diet and proper hygiene. With other physicians, he founded a school of medicine which followed a common medical doctrine. These physicians developed new theories from established discoveries and shared ideas with one another. Hippocrates understood the importance of careful observation and classification, and believed it was impossible to understand part of the human body without understanding the whole. Only then, he believed, could a physician proceed to diagnose. This was the central point of his teaching. He said:

'The life so short, the craft so long to learn.'

Hippocrates and his fellow physicians swore an oath, which doctors the world over still swear today. (See page 43 — an 1850 translation.)

FOUR

The Greek theatre

The story of the theatre dates from earliest antiquity; it was created long before the great dramatists achieved their successes.

The people celebrated the grape harvest at annual festivals and paid homage to the god, Dionysus. An altar would be set up in a clearing and men and women would dance and sing accompanied by lyre and flute. The men were called satyrs and the women, maenads. If they danced particularly well they were given a goat, an animal sacred to Dionysus, as a prize. Their dance was called a *tragodoi* (goat song) from which the modern word 'tragedy' is derived. The satyrs and maenads were called the chorus, and they offered wine to the god as they danced and cavorted around his altar, drinking quite a bit themselves! Sometimes revellers dressed as goats, pinning on horns, hooves and tails. These half-men half-goat merrymakers were immortalised on many vases and frescoes.

As time progressed, the songs of the chorus were recorded by poets who added to them their own interpretations. One of these poets, Thespis, actually took the part of the god Dionysus and spoke to the chorus. This was such a success that he wrote more lines for himself, thus becoming the first actor in history. (Our own word 'thespian' comes from his name.)

Some fifty years later, the great dramatist Aeschylus wrote a play with lines for an individual performer in the chorus, so dialogue was being used more widely. The ancient rituals were now giving way to the play itself which began to have a recognisable plot.

Dionysus was no longer the only god to be celebrated in this way; other gods and heroes were also featured in plays. The chorus was reduced from 50 to 12 performers and this allowed more space on the stage for special effects. A device called a *mechane* was used for hoisting the actors up and down on the stage, so that a miraculous entry of a god direct from heaven had a marvellous effect on the audience and solved many production difficulties. Pebbles were

45

Head of the wine god, from the theatre of Dionysus, (opened in 543 BC), on the southern slopes of the acropolis.

poured out of a jar into a large bronze vessel to emulate the sound of thunder, or lead balls dropped on a sheet of tightly stretched leather. Lightning was cleverly staged by painting a light coloured flash on a plank of wood against a dark background and hurling it into a receptacle below!

The actors would be kept very busy rushing backwards and forwards, changing costumes and characters. Masks were used to communicate feelings and the age or sex of the characters. A mask could transform a happy old man into a sad young woman. There were no female actors. The masks themselves were made of light wood or stiffened material. They covered the whole head, and were works of art in their own right. The mouth area was always large so that the actor's voice could be clearly heard, and the masks were sometimes topped with an elaborate wig. The actor would always cover his face; a naked face was considered sacrilege. The collection of masks was large, depicting all the gods and heroes — so that an actor could have as many as 45 masks at his disposal.

The expressions on the masks were exaggerated so that everyone in the theatre could follow the action of the play. The actors wore shoes with thick soles to increase their height, they padded their shoulders and bodies for extra width and wore robes with large sleeves to appear larger than life.

There is evidence to suggest that the tragic actors did not move as much as comic actors on stage, relying on vocal expression and elaborate gestures to convey their points. This was a sensible solution, since the perilous height of their shoes and the weight of their masks must have put them in danger of toppling over and even falling off the stage!

Epidaurus Theatre (fourth century) is still used today. The acoustics are perfect for all 14,000 seats.

In the early days, when the theatre was first developing, the performers would prepare themselves in a make-shift tent called a *skeneon* which was just behind the dancing area. In time the skeneon was built in stone and gradually developed into a building with a portico, which was used by the actors to make dramatic entrances. The skeneon was the permanent back-drop for the stage which was now a round, stone, paved area. Theatres were built in natural depressions in hillsides, forming amphitheatres. At the beginning the audience would sit on hewn earth, but gradually the seating improved to wood and then to the more durable materials of stone or marble.

The theatre was considered an important part of cultural life in Greece, and on festival days all the shops, schools, businesses, workshops and even the law courts were closed. Performances started at dawn and lasted all day. Those too poor to be able to afford a ticket were subsidised by the State and their wages could be reimbursed.

In Athens two forms of drama came to dominate the Dionysian theatre, comedy and tragedy. The Lenaea festival (January-February), reserved for celebrating weddings, was devoted to comedies while the city of Dionysia festival (March-April) was devoted to tragedy.

Euripides 485-406 BC was a contemporary of Sophocles, and the first realist among the great dramatic writers. He allowed his characters their human failings, and his realistic and sometimes pessimistic view of men and gods led him into conflict with the authorities. He was forced to leave Athens for Macedonia where he remained until his death. He wrote over 90 plays of which 19 have survived.

Aristophanes 450-385 BC came to prominence during the long Peloponnesian war, and gave a little light relief to the Athenians with his satire and comedy. He ridiculed the entire establishment, and no prominent figure was safe from his pen. He wrote over 20 comedies but only 11 are known to us today.

After the Roman invasion, Greek drama was nearly forgotten. Roman playwrights took precedence, but in the sixteenth century, interest in the classical Greek theatre revived and some of the plays were printed for the first time. Scholars and artists in Florence started to recreate the old spectacles of actors and chorus. This was the beginning of Grand Opera as we know it.

(Opposite) Top: *The Parthenon, Athens (5th century BC)*
Bottom: *The monasteries of Meteora, Thessaly, spectacularly perched atop these great monolithic rocks.*

FIVE

The Olympic story

Nearly every city staged its own games in honour of the gods, but the most popular were the Nemean games at Argolis and the Isthmian games at Corinth, held every two years; the Olympic games at Olympia and the Pythian games at Delphi, held every four years. These events drew athletes from all over Greece, each one competing as an individual. There was a fierce competitive spirit, which possibly explains why there were no team events. Political differences were put aside and a truce in wartime was considered sacred. The honour of the games was supreme.

The greatest and oldest of the games were the Olympic games held at Olympia. They began in 776 BC and lasted until 393 AD. Olympia was not a city but a group of temples, shrines, priests' houses, offices and arenas. People travelled from all over Greece and beyond to witness this great spectacle, and set up temporary homes in the surrounding countryside. There was an air of festivity with vendors selling anything from food to horses. Poets, orators and artists came to entertain, teach or sell their skills. Jugglers, musicians and acrobats all contributed to the lighthearted and festive atmosphere, vying with each other in their own competitions. It was important to be seen and heard at Olympia. Perhaps after the games and back in their own city, their talents would have been held in greater esteem for having performed at Olympia.

Some really enthusiastic spectators would arrive early to watch the athletes in their final stages of training and speculate on possible winners. There was a colonnade some 200 yards long by the Gymnasium, where runners would practise their sprints. There were special rooms for athletes, with facilities for washing and resting. Here the young competitors could be seen scraping each other's

(**Opposite**) *Aghios Nicholaos, Crete.*

*Ancient Olympia, Peloponnese (above) where the Panhellenic
Games were held every four years; and the stadium, Athens
(below), built in 1895 for the first modern Olympic games. The
stadium holds 10,000 people.*

bodies with an instrument called a *strigil*. This was to remove the olive oil and sweat, leaving the skin supple and clean. Each competitor had to take an oath that he was qualified both legally and physically to compete. He had to be a native of Greece and a freeman — no slaves were entitled to compete. He also must have faithfully performed the required discipline set out in the rules.

The athletes' training course was hard and lasted for ten months. The final month was a rigorous course of exercises in the Gymnasium at Olympia. It is little wonder that the Greek word for this — *agonas,* meaning 'hard struggle' — became the English word, 'agony'.

In most cases athletes competed naked and barefoot. They took a pride in the physical appearance of their bodies and abhorred obesity. The main events of the games were running, boxing and wrestling, charioteering, jumping and bareback horse riding.

The opening event of the Olympic games was a four-horse chariot race. As many as 35 to 40 chariots lined up for this spectacular event. The course was over eight miles long and the galloping horses and chariots swerved dangerously round the stone posts of the ground. There were many spills and collisions and inevitable injuries both to men and horses. Very few who started the race finished. The noise must have been deafening.

The victor's crown went to the owner of the chariot and horses and not the charioteer. Rich men were able to enter more than one chariot, thus standing a better chance of winning.

Wrestling was also very popular. Wrestlers, their bodies brought to a peak of strength and fitness, fought in one of the most brutal of the recorded sports. The contestants punched, kicked and strangled each other; nothing was barred save gouging and biting, and it was considered unfair to break an opponents fingers, but otherwise it seems to have been a free-for-all. A contestant would raise a finger when he conceded defeat.

Women were strictly barred from the games although there is a story of one young mother who, proud of her son's abilities, wanted to see him perform so, disguised as a man, she slipped into the games among the other spectators. However, she was discovered and arrested, but later pardoned when her son became an Olympic victor.

The winners of the Olympic games won only garlands of wild laurel leaves; victory was reward enough, but the prestige and ensuing benefits were endless. In their own cities they would be given a hero's welcome and paraded with pride through the streets. Poems would be written about their achievements and statues raised in their honour. They would be exempt from paying taxes and often given great sums of money from grateful townspeople. It was indeed a worthwhile victory.

It must not be forgotten that the Olympic games were also a religious festival. The great temple of Zeus stood in the centre of the *Altis* or sacred precinct of Zeus, which housed a giant statue of the god, considered one of the seven wonders of the ancient world. The statue, in a sitting position, measured about 40 feet high, the head being near the roof of the temple. It was made of gold and ivory with a wooden core and was the work of the famous sculptor Phidias who also was responsible for the great statue of Athena in the Parthenon.

The Olympic games continued to take place every four years, long after the Roman occupation, but slowly, the old happy atmosphere of festivity, patriotism and honouring the gods deteriorated into a corrupt and debasing spectacle. Cheating and bribery were rife. Theodosius I stopped the festival in 393 AD, and the beautiful site of Olympia was left silent and empty for over a thousand years.

In 1896 the games were revived, thanks to the efforts of a French sports enthusiast, Baron de Coubertin. They have since been held in different countries every four years, except during the First and Second World Wars.

SIX

Lemons with everything

The first meal I ate in Greece was at a small taverna in Crete. In the centre of the table was a large plate full of cut lemons. In amazement I watched my escort, a typical Cretan with a large moustache and an aura of proud masculinity, enthusiastically swamp every dish that was placed before us with lemon juice. The *meze* (Greek hors d'oeuvre) absorbed two lemons, the lamb kebab two more, the salad one, and the melon at the end of the meal, another. Used in such a haphazard and careless way, squeezing at random and drenching everything, seemed odd, if not extravagant. With my Yorkshire upbringing lemons were bought only when someone was suffering from a bad cold or sore throat, or occasionally they would be added to a capricious strawberry jam that refused to set. The meal, however, tasted delicious, but the water I consumed for the rest of the day left me feeling rather like a sunken tug boat. Since that time I have become a lemon addict and add it to any dish at the drop of a hat. 'Lemons with everything' is now a catch-phrase with all my friends!

Lemons are vital to modern Greek cooking but exactly when the lemon habit began seems to be a mystery, as it was unknown in cooking or as an edible fruit (except as medicine) in the ancient world. Lemons were taken to Spain when the Crusaders discovered them growing in Palestine, and it was from Spain that they were introduced to the rest of Europe. There is no doubt that lemons play an important part in the health of the Greek nation. They are rich in vitamin C and have important medicinal qualities. The peel is also valuable, containing generous quantities of aromatic oils which can be obtained either by compressing or distillation and are used in perfumes, pastry making and the manufacture of confectionery. The peel is also specially prepared with sugar as a tasty crystalized sweet. But now we will return to pre-lemon days.

Since ancient times the Greeks have been interested in food and

Cooking the souvlaki over a charcoal fire.

even in the earliest writings there is frequent mention of feats of great culinary skill. The philosopher Archestratus, whose 'gastrology' was a culinary masterpiece, travelled widely in search of new recipes and ideas. He recorded his recipes for posterity around the year 350 BC, and some people maintain they are still is use today!

Herbs contribute to the delicate flavours of many dishes and Hippocrates, the father of medicine, frequently used them for his cures. It has been claimed that he used over 400 different types of herbs! Chervil, tasting rather like caraway, was used to cure hiccups, and parsley was a useful remedy for the excesses of wine. Dill was chewed by senators as they indulged in speeches lasting many hours, and theatre audiences used it to keep them awake during over-long plays when they ran the risk of nodding off! Today cherries are still considered to have valuable medicinal qualities; the flesh being good for the blood and stomach and the stones, when boiled in water, produce a liquid that can dissolve kidney stones — or so they say!

In modern Greece, eating is very much a social event. Groups of people, families and friends, pour into the small cafés and tavernas, particularly on Saturday evenings, to drink, eat and enjoy themselves. The atmosphere of a taverna is one of pleasant chaotic order. Meals are an informal affair and not set strictly to courses as in the rest of Europe. Food tends to reach the table as and when it is cooked, so a meal usually takes two or three hours, or even longer to complete. This leisurely way of eating is, I feel, much better for the digestion and makes the meal the social event that it is.

It is customary and, indeed, expected to walk into a taverna kitchen to select the meat or fish you desire. With great pride, the proprietor will fling open his fridge door to reveal trays of fresh steaks and kebabs and rows of gleaming fish, their eyes still wide with indignation. Once, when I was inspecting my dinner, a large pincer snapped, narrowly missing my thumb. Startled, I tipped the tray over and half a kilo of furious lobster scuttled out of the kitchen and made its escape, lurching over the foot of an elderly lady customer with a forkful of *bourboni* half way to her mouth. The ensuing confusion left me with a very red face.

Usually when you choose your meat or fish, you buy it by weight and not by portion as we would expect to do. The wine is brought to the table accompanied by tumblers which need refilling at rapid intervals. I have never discovered why such small glasses are used, but one philosophical Greek maintained that the wine tasted better. Fruit is always seasonal, each variety being available according to

Heraklion market, Crete: the cheese seller (above), and (below) fresh fruit and vegetables on sale

the agricultural calendar. (The nectarines and cherries are the sweetest I have tasted anywhere in the world — absolutely delightful.)

The atmosphere of a taverna usually reflects the personality of the proprietor. Every Greek is a frustrated politician and every other an undiscovered philosopher! If his favourite subject in politics is being discussed by a customer, uninvited he will gladly participate, not hesitating to disagree and thumping his fist on the table to make his

his point clear. He will then depart, the best of friends and glad to have been able to solve the problem! Regardless of age or bulk, he might also display his prowess as a dancer, leaping into the air, clicking his heels and snapping his fingers to the music, with great agility and not a little unresponsive to encouragement. But above all he is an individual.

A dear Cretan friend, a fanatic sailor, once told me that if I wanted to eat excellent fish, I must try George's taverna. It was, he said, just outside the village of Elounda; I couldn't miss it, there was a blue sign. Now when a Greek gives directions and says 'you can't miss it', it's a safe bet that his directions are as accurate as his time keeping. (Greek time is a notoriously flexible business, noon being anywhere between 2 and 4 pm.) So with rather fragile hopes, I set off. It was no surprise that I could find no trace of George or his taverna, and the only sign I could see was a long abandoned road works sign. After touring the area for half an hour, I caught a glimpse of a blue sign away from the road, down a rough dirt track heading towards the sea. Running the risk of removing the car sump, I drove towards the sign, carefully avoiding the donkeys and goats that were enjoying their lunch in the middle of the road. George's taverna appeared, hugging the water-line with its own small jetty. Then I remembered: Ted only ever approached the taverna by boat!

I had been warned of George's somewhat temperamental nature. If he felt inclined, he rose early to catch the fish for the day's meals. If not, the restaurant was closed. If you caught him on a bad day, asking for lunch was like playing Russian roulette. Also a great deal depended upon whether he liked your face. So far no one had taken offence at mine, so I parked the car, coughed my way through the ensuing dust cloud and entered the taverna.

The place was empty except for two men playing *tavli,* a form of backgammon, very popular with the Greeks. I bade them 'Yassas' and sat down. One of the men was definitely George; Ted's description was very accurate. Apparently the game was more interesting than I was — so I waited. By this time I was getting very hungry and even more thirsty, so politely I asked if I could have some food. 'Sorry no fiss today,' said George in his lovely Greek accent, and carried on throwing the dice. I remembered that Ted had said to mention his name, which might produce some fish. This I did. George looked up sharply, his face broke out into a broad grin and I was quickly hauled off to the kitchens to choose from the morning's catch. Since then I have visited George's taverna many times, and have spent many happy hours in his company. He plays the *bouzouki* with extraordinary talent and when the spirit moves him dances magnificently.

One clear spring day in April, I was driving leisurely along the main road heading for George's taverna thinking of fresh *barbounia* (a small, delicious, orange-coloured fish) and *mizithra meli* (a special soft cheese topped with honey). The car window was open and I could smell the fresh sweet air, scented by thousands of wild flowers scattered over the stony hillside. The multi-coloured faces of the anemones and cyclamen and the bright red heads of the poppies gave a festive mood to the countryside. Momentarily forgetting lunch, I drew the car into the side of the road, turned off the engine and clambered out. A soft breeze gently moved the clumps of tall yellow daisies by the side of the road. A lark was singing, so high as not to be visible. I breathed in deeply; the smell of the countryside was like a narcotic and I felt the sheer joy of being alive. I stood for several minutes in soundless rapture. My gaze swept the panoramic view of the hillside and valley across to the fretted coastline, where white tipped waves gently nibbled the shore. Far below an old donkey, with bowed head, stood tethered to an olive tree, patiently waiting for his midday meal.

A pang of hunger nudged my reflections and I hastened back to the car. To my dismay the front near-side tyre was flat, squashed on top of a nail-ridden board. Feeling as competent as a butcher trying to perform brain surgery, I peered into the car boot to see if there was anything there resembling a jack. The boot appeared to be empty except for the spare wheel. My heart sank. I suddenly realised I had not seen another human being for well over an hour.

I was just about to see if anything was concealed under the bonnet when I heard the slow chugging of a laboured engine. Rounding the corner came the old village bus crowned with two boxes of chickens, several crates of assorted vegetables and a large box of lemons. I ran into the middle of the road frantically waving my arms. The bus ground to a halt and the driver slowly climbed out. When I pointed to the flat tyre, he immediately took charge of the situation and promptly selected four young men from among the passengers for the task of changing the wheel. With good humoured smiles they set about the dirty job. The boot was full of hidden tools and, ignoring the busdriver's, expert advice and instructions, they soon had the punctured wheel off and the spare one on. Before I had time to say anything in my uncertain Greek, they had all jumped back on the bus and with shouts of 'Kalo taxithi' (safe journey) pulled slowly away. Gratefully I waved and shouted 'Efharisto, efharisto' before inhaling the sweet smell of

A proud villager of Elefsis shows off her cockerel.

black diesel fumes!

It was 2.30 pm by the time the taverna's blue sign appeared in the distance. George's sad face told me the bad news. That morning his boat engine had stopped three times. It was, he said, a bad omen; there was nothing he could do but abandon the fishing trip and go back to bed! I was, however, more fortunate on my next visit.

On a perfect summer evening I was sitting with a group of friends having just enjoyed George's marvellous fish when a young man entered the taverna with a *bouzouki* under his arm. He started to play the old Greek tunes of fifty years ago. I remember looking out over the sea, there was a full bright moon which had illuminated the dark water with a myriad of shimmering lights. As the music progressed I suddenly understood why the Greeks felt so passionately about their freedom and country. The music filled every corner of the taverna and beyond. George stood in the middle of the floor; raising his arms, his body swayed and his fingers started to snap to the slow rhythm of the *Khasapiko*. I always feel that when a Greek is moved to dance, he bares his soul to the world. With shouts of 'Opah' from the enthusiastic patrons, plates started to fly across the floor, smashing at his feet. This is a sign of appreciation and soon the floor was littered with broken pottery. (A keen eye is, of course, kept on who breaks what. There is a moment of reckoning at the end of the evening!)

SEVEN

For the chef

Here is a small selection of my favourite Greek recipes which are both economical and delicious. I hope you will enjoy trying them. Make sure you have a large stock of lemons! *Kali orexe!* (Good appetite!)

Soupa avgolemono
(egg and lemon soup)

2 pints good chicken stock
2 oz uncooked rice
2 eggs

salt to taste
juice of one lemon

Cook the rice in the stock until tender. Beat the eggs thoroughly then gradually add the lemon juice. Take two cups of the hot broth and add them slowly to the egg and lemon mixture, making a sauce. Just before serving the soup, add the sauce to the broth stirring all the time and add the salt to taste. Heat up slowly once more and allow to stand for 5 minutes.

Beans of all shapes and sizes, fresh or dried, make a delicious and nourishing meal. Eaten either as part of a *meze* (Greek hors-d'oeuvre) or as a main meal fortified with chopped cheese and hunks of bread, their versatility is unlimited. It must be remembered that **if ever red kidney beans are used, they must be boiled rapidly for a minimum of 10 minutes** before any ingredients are added.

Fassolia yiyandes plaki
(butter beans with onions and tomatoes)

1lb dried butter beans
2 medium chopped onions
1 chopped clove of garlic
2 chopped tomatoes (peeled)

1 tablespoon chopped mint
juice of ½ a lemon
salt and pepper
oil for frying

Soak the beans overnight. Cook them rapidly for 10 minutes in the same water then drain. Replace with fresh salted water and cook until tender adding a tablespoonful of chopped onions during the final stages of cooking. Fry the remaining onions, garlic and tomatoes in the oil. Add the mint and lemon juice and transfer this mixture into the bean pan. Let this simmer gently for a further 30 minutes. A point to remember: as the mixture thickens check that the bottom does not stick and burn. This recipe can be varied using different beans (but see page 61) and by adding celery or carrots.

Kolokithakia yahni
(stewed marrow)

½ vegetable marrow cubed
   and peeled*
2 chopped onions
2 large chopped tomatoes
   (peeled)
teaspoon mixed herbs

oil for frying
salt to taste
juice of ½ lemon

Fry the onions. Take a large pan and place alternate layers of marrow, onions and tomatoes. Add lemon juice and herbs and sufficient salted water to cover vegetables and allow to simmer without a lid until cooked. (*If the marrow is young it will not need peeling.)

*A speciality of Simi in the Dodecanese: freshly caught octopus.
It will be beaten on the rocks to tenderise it before cooking.*

Arni paithakia sto harti *or* Kleftico
(roast lamb chops in parcels)

The origins of this dish go back to the Turkish occupation when life was very hard. Meat was very difficult to obtain. Greeks living in the countryside supplemented their diet occasionally by stealing the odd sheep from the Turks, hence the name *Kleftico,* meaning stolen. (Our own word kleptomania comes from the Greek word *kleptes,* meaning thief.) To avoid detection, they cooked the meat in small kilns to eliminate the smell.

Wipe the chops and lay each one on a piece of tinfoil large enough to make a parcel. Sprinkle with salt, pepper, marjoram, a little lemon juice and coat liberally with grated hard cheese. (I use parmesan). Place in a moderate oven and cook for 1¼ hours. Open up the parcels and give them a further fifteen minutes.

Arni kapama me patates
(braised lamb with potatoes)

2lb lamb neck chops	1 pint water
1lb potatoes, quartered	salt to taste
12 peppercorns	1 tablespoon flour
juice of one lemon	oil for frying

Trim the fat off the meat and fry until cooked. Add water, flour for thickening, lemon juice, salt, peppercorns and potatoes. Let it simmer until meat is very tender and potatoes are cooked and starting to fall.

Arni me fassolia
(lamb with beans)

½lb dried haricot beans	2 cloves of garlic
1lb cubed lamb	juice of ½ lemon
2 large onions	salt
3 tomatoes (peeled)	oil for frying

Soak the beans overnight. Fry the onions and garlic in a little oil.

A traditional oven. Wood is burnt inside to heat the stones, and the ashes are then scraped to one side. Once the food is inserted the door is closed to retain the heat. Several villagers may share one oven.

Put all the ingredients except the tomatoes with the beans and simmer until the meat and beans are tender. Add the chopped tomatoes and cook for a further 15 minutes.

Dolmathes
(stuffed vine leaves)

½lb minced meat
1 large onion
1 tablespoon chopped mint
1 tablespoon tomato puree
juice of ½ lemon

salt and pepper
1 tablespoon olive oil
4 oz uncooked rice
1 pint good stock

Many shops stock vine leaves in brine either loose or in packets. But if these cannot be found cabbage or spinach leaves can be used. Chop onions and fry gently in oil. Add meat and fry for a further 10 minutes. Then mix in the mint, puree, salt, pepper, lemon juice and uncooked rice. If the vine leaves are in brine, wash them carefully and place a spoonful of mixture into each leaf to make a loose parcel, allowing space for the rice to swell. Put each parcel into a pan and pour the stock over them. Place an old plate, a little smaller than the pan, on top of the *dolmathes*. This ensures that they do not fall apart. Open one *dolmathe* and test the rice after 20 minutes. Make sure the *dolmathes* do not stick and burn.

Kotopoulo psito
(roast chicken)

4 chicken pieces
4 potatoes
2 tomatoes (peeled)
1 clove garlic

1 onion
salt and pepper
juice of one lemon
oil for coating

Place the chicken pieces in a roasting dish and brush with olive oil and rub with garlic. Chop onion, tomatoes and potatoes and arrange around the chicken pieces. Brush with oil and sprinkle with salt, pepper and lemon juice. Pour in ½ teacup of water and roast

open in a moderate oven for 1¼ hours or until well cooked, turning
the vegetables half way through.

Taramosalata

6 oz fish roe
10 oz dry white bread crumbs
1 small onion finely chopped

5 fl oz olive oil
juice of two lemons

You can use tinned cod's roe, found in many delicatessens. Put the
roe, oil and onion into the blender and blend until smooth. Soak
the bread crumbs and squeeze water out. Add this, together with
lemon juice, to the mixture in the blender and blend until smooth.
If the flavour is too strong, this can be diluted by adding more
breadcrumbs. For a very special occasion, caviar can be used.

Known as 'the cradle of Greek wine' the island of Paros in the heart of the Cyclades has also been famed throughout the ages for its Parian marble.

EIGHT

The grape and the vine

'Wine is very appropriate to man, in good health and
in illness, and should be administered opportunely and
with measure, according to individual constitution.'

Hippocrates (460-377 BC)

In ancient times, Greek wines were sold not only in Greece but also
in the market-places of the known world. We know that wine was
traded for cereals in Egypt, for silver in Andalusia, for wood in the
Caucasus, for metals in Armenia and for wool in Spain. From the
thirteenth to the eleventh centuries BC, the development of the
vineyards was at its height. The vine was grown much as it is today,
spaced along parallel lines.

Greek mythology is strewn with references to wine or 'nectar' and
great poets like Homer, Hesiodus and Pindarus praised its qualities
in their odes. Aristophanes, the Athenian genius of comedy,
delighted his audiences with scenes where the slaves stole into their
master's cellars to get drunk at their ease. It is little wonder that
Dionysus was honoured as the god of wine; according to the myths,
he invented wine whilst sojourning on Mount Nysa *(nysa* is a
homeric word meaning 'a hill with trees'). Hera, Zeus's wife, hated
Dionysus and his vine cup, opposing the ritual use of wine and the
excesses of the cult that spread from Thrace to Athens, Corinth,
Sicyon, Delphi and other civilised cities.

But in the early·sixth century BC, the cult was approved and an
official Dionysiac feast was founded. Dionysus and his wine were
held to have been accepted in heaven. The wine was the tenth tree
of the sacral tree year and its month corresponded with September
when the vintage feast took place.

The cult of Dionysus was closely linked with the theatre and the
'seat of honour' in the auditorium was reserved for the high priest
of Dionysus. Other priests claimed 50 of the 67 front row seats

followed by officials, guests of honour and ordinary citizens. Dionysus offered his followers eternal salvation and there is little doubt that the inspiration he gave to the great poets, sculptors, philosophers and painters won immortality for his cult, as this quotation observes:

> 'The cult of Dionysus has considerably influenced
> the development of religion, poetry and arts in
> Greece, and has contributed to the introduction of a
> sense of mystery in religion; of the feeling of nature
> in lyric poetry; of impassioned movement in
> sculpture as shown in the Dionysiac reliefs. Lastly
> drama, literature and poetry were born from his
> religious rites.'

Today, wine is a more scientific business. There are eight chief wine districts in Greece, and the Peloponnese is the most important. In Corinth, vineyards start from the coast and spread up to a height of 800 metres. The Nemean region gives a dry full-bodied red wine called Nemea or High Nemea according to the altitude of the vineyard, and well deserves its name, the 'Blood of Hercules'. Patras is best known for its fortified wines, Mavrodaphne and Muscat of Patras.

In the centre of the Peloponnese, at an altitude of 650 metres and surrounding the ancient ruins of Mantinea, grow the Moschofilero vines, giving a well-balanced fruity white wine called Mantenia.

The region of Attica which is in the wine growing region of Central Greece, is the warmest and driest of Greece, with stony arid soil. A range of important white wines come from the Savatiano grape. The wines produced from this stock, which is resistent to drought, vary greatly according to the place of production. Attica produces 65 per cent of the renowned Retsina, one of the best known Greek wines. It is made like other wines, the only difference being that, before fermentation, pine resin is added, thus giving it its distinctive flavour. The alleged antiseptic quality of resin goes back to antiquity when resinated wines were first made. At that time wine was stored and transported in jars and amphorae. As these were not airtight, the wine quickly deteriorated. Eventually the people learned to seal the jars with a mixture of plaster and resin. Being airtight, the wine lasted longer. The better preservation of the wine was naturally attributed to the resin.

Crete is an important wine-producing area, coming third after Peloponnese and mainland Greece. Crossing the island from the east to west we first come to the vineyards of Sitia with medium

Sculptured frieze of the progress of the wine god, from the Theatre of Dionysus (opened in 534 BC) on the southern slopes of the Acropolis.

production from the Liatico vine, a small grape which is considered to be the forerunner of the Black Vine of Corinth. Sitia (red) is a strong and full-bodied wine of Superior Quality. Moving further west is the Heraklion district. Just outside Heraklion is Knossos, the ancient palace of the Minoan civilisation where a flourishing wine trade lasted for many centuries. Today, most of the wine production is exported, coming from the red Kotsifali vine which is cultivated almost exclusively on the island of Crete, and the Mantilari vine which is a familiar vine of the Aegean islands. The wines are strong and full-bodied with a distinct taste. The Liatico grape is cultivated in the hilly areas of Daphnes. The fortified wine bearing the name of this region is very like the wine of Sitia and is also a wine of Superior Quality. These wines recall the famous Malvasia or Malmsey wine which, according to legend, was made in huge jars in the palace of Minos from a recipe given to the king of Crete by the Delphic Oracle. This wine is supposed to symbolise wisdom. In the district of Chania, in the extreme west of the island, the red Romeikon vine is cultivated almost exclusively.

The Ionian islands produce a good selection of wine including Mavrodaphne of Cephalonia (red), Muscat of Cephalonia (white) and the popular Robola of Cephalonia (white).

Since ancient times Rhodes produced a large quantity of wine and this was exported in amphorae. The ancient potters would stamp the name of the wine followed by a bunch of grapes, which was and still is their trademark. Rhodes, one of the Aegean group of wine producers, today owes its fame to the light, white table-wines from the mountainous regions where the Athiri vine is cultivated, from which Ilios, a fruity dry white wine, comes. A red wine, Chevalier de Rhodes, comes from the Amorgiano vine and combines delicacy with strength. Both wines are 'Appellation of Origin' status. The sweet white Muscadet of Rhodes and Trani Muscat are made only in limited quantities and come from the southern vineyards. The Muscat of Rhodes has 'Appellation of Origin' status.

Santorini produces the unusual aperitif called Santorini from the Assyrtiko and Aidani grapes.

Paros in the Cyclades, the 'cradle of Greek wine', has a particularly mild climate and has produced wine for three thousand years. Paros (red) comes from the Mandilaria grape whose vines are pruned in a basket shape. The shoots and leaves make the outer wall and the grapes grow protected inside. Paros has an 'Appellation of Origin' status.

Macedonia and Thrace are famous for their crimson wines. Despite the destruction suffered in their vineyards by phylloxera about fifty years ago, production is as high as in Crete today. Of the red wines produced here, the wines of Naoussa and Amynteon are the best known with an 'Appellation of Origin of Superior Quality'. Naoussa wines are amongst the most prestigious exported from Greece and were among a list of only 15 officially designated 'Superior Quality' under EEC regulations.

I have left the famous wines of Samos until last. Samos derived its name from the Phoenician word Sama meaning high. It is a very mountainous island with its two main peaks, Karakateus and Ambelos, rising to a height of 1570 and 1160 metres respectively. The Samos soil is perfectly suited to the growing of vines. An ancient proverb claims that 'even fowls bear milk on Samos'. The Muscat grape is grown throughout Greece but is most successful on Samos where it is believed to have originated. The wines are sweet, semi-sweet and dry, but the most famous is the Muscat of Samos. The vines, cultivated on terraces, stretch along the northern shore from Karlovassi to the town of Samos. The grapes are picked by hand and the wine stored and aged in large oak vats. It is said that

Hippocrates recommended the wine for his patients during convalescence.

There is a story about a mythological tyrant called Agaios who, it is said, took the grape to Samos. He was very harsh to the local population, making them work hard in his vineyards. One day, one of his slaves told Agaios that he would die before he tasted the wine which was to be produced. Angry, Agaios made his people work even harder and, as a result, the vineyards yielded a particularly good harvest. When the time came for Agaios to taste the first of his wine at an official ceremony, he invited the slave who had prophesied his death to come and watch the first wine being drunk. Cup in hand he ridiculed the slave for his prediction, but the slave, undeterred, quietly retorted: 'There is a lot of space between the cup and the lip.' Before Agaios could reply, a servant rushed up to his master and reported that a mad bull was running wild among the vines. Agaios put his cup down and went to the vineyard to kill the unfortunate animal. He never returned to taste his wine!

Enjoying the good things in life.

73

Whether this story is fact or fiction, it is well known that the great Pythagoras indulged (maybe over indulged) in the sweet wine of his birthplace while philosophising and creating the basis of modern mathematics. Anakreon, who probably wrote more poems about wine than any other poet, declared that Samos wines were definitely the best.

The chapter would not be complete if mention was not made of *ouzo,* the national drink of Greece. This is a clear spirit distilled from grapes, with a mixture of aniseed and fennel added. Some people manage to drink it neat but it is more palatable mixed with water and ice. It is very pleasant drunk as an aperitif and with a side-plate of tomatoes, cucumber, cheese and olives.

NINE

A calendar of Greek traditions, past and present

As has been said in the introduction, the past and present come together, linked by the Church, to exist harmoniously throughout Greece. The Orthodox calendar is faithfully observed and rituals, reaching back through the centuries, still play an important role in the lives of the people.

New Year's Day, 1 January

The first of January is St Basil's day and is very important in the Greek calendar, each district having its own customs and rituals. The 'first person to enter the house' on New Year's Day is the most significant part of the festival. In some parts of Greece it is believed that the first person should be the master of the house, or his eldest son, or a 'lucky child'. (A lucky child usually means a child whose parents are both living.)

On the island of Amorgos, the chosen person must be a member of the family and he must be returning from church with a small icon in his hand. He takes two steps into the house saying, 'Come in, good luck' and then two steps backwards saying, 'Out, bad luck'. This must be done three times. The third time he enters the house, he throws a pomegranate to the ground so that it splits open. Then all the members of the family dip a finger in honey and suck it so that the new year may be as sweet as honey. This is followed by eating boiled wheat in St Basil's name.

At Lassithi in Crete, the first stranger to enter the house must bring a large stone, place it in the middle of the room, sit upon it and say 'Good day to you, happy new month. Blessings upon your poultry, your lambs and your goats. May your hen sit on her eggs, may your cow give birth to a calf, may your she-ass give birth to a mule. Female lambs and kids to you, and male children. And may gold the weight of this stone enter your house.' The stranger is then offered sweetmeats.

On New Year's Day morning in the island of Karpathos, a white dog is brought into the house and fed with *baklava*, a sweet cake. This is believed to give the household strength of body and spirit.

The dinner table is another important feature of the New Year's festivities; it must be richly laden with food which symbolises abundance and prosperity.

In all parts of Greece, it is the custom to cut the *Vassilopitta*, or St Basil's Cake. It is made of milk, eggs, butter and sugar. A coin is slipped into the cake after it has been baked, and the person who receives the coin will be the lucky person of the year.

Sometimes the housewife bakes a special cake for the oxen, both on Christmas Eve and on New Year's Eve. In the island of Karpathos, this cake is called *Vouopitta*, or oxen pie, and in Skyros it is even given the shape of a harness. This cake or pie is broken into crumbs and mixed with salt and then fed to the oxen.

It is a popular belief that St Basil comes down to earth and visits every house on New Year's Day, so each household gets ready for his visit. At Aghiassos, in Lesbos, the heavily laden table is left all night so that St Basil may sit and eat. A long log is placed upright in the grate so that he can step down the chimney without difficulty. On the island of Skyros, a tray is set with a bowl of water, two dishes of pancakes or some other sweet, a pomegranate and a pestle or stone, so that St Basil may 'refresh himself and sweeten his tongue'. The house will then remain 'fresh and sweet' all the year round. For the rural population, St Basil is believed to be a farmer and on New Year's Eve he is expected to visit the farm animals. Before nightfall the animals are brushed and groomed. Their fodder is mixed with wheat and oats and each animal gets its share of *Vassilopitta*. St Basil then comes to ask them if they fare well and if they are looked after properly.

Another custom that takes place in the farming areas is when the shepherds and sheep-owners welcome the New Year in the sheepfolds and cut the *Vassilopitta*. At Hassia, in western Macedonia, the wives of shepherds and cattle-breeders get up before midnight on New Year's Eve to bake the *Vassilopitta*. A small twig is inserted symbolising the sheepfold. When the cake is ready the master of the house takes it to the fold; he also takes some wine, food and bread and wishes his shepherd a happy New Year and 'may the sheep increase to a thousand'. They both sit and drink, eat and sing. The one who gets the piece of cake containing the twig will be the bearer of the sheep's good luck. The twig is then buried somewhere safe inside the pen. The celebration goes on until day break.

In some parts of Greece olive or laurel branches are hung at the front door or gate. This is an old Byzantine custom. Six olive and six laurel branches are also hung under the icons, while a member of the family says, 'Come in good year, go out bad year'. In Sinope in Pontus, it is customary to hang an olive branch with forty or fifty leaves, studded with hazelnuts, over the fire-place where it remains all year. On New Year's Eve the old branch is replaced by a new one. Byzantium inherited this custom from Rome.

There are many superstitions about what must and must not be done on New Year's Day. One must not cry or lose anything as this will continue throughout the year. No black dog is allowed in the house but a white one is welcomed and given cake. It is considered bad luck to break a mirror on New Year's Day. It is also the day for people to visit each other, exchanging gifts and good wishes.

In some parts of Greece the windows and doors are left open all day so that anyone, friend or stranger, may enter and receive his share of cake.

Epiphany, 6 January

Epiphany is the day when Christ was baptised by St John the Baptist in the river Jordan and it is a day of great celebration in Greece. On this day the waters are blessed and it is believed that all evil spirits depart from the earth and that the waters of the sea become sweet and drinkable. The 'Blessing of the Waters' begins in church on the eve of Epiphany. After the service the priest goes in procession through the town or village, visiting each house in order to bless it, sprinkling all the rooms with a sprig of basil dipped in holy water.

On the eve of Epiphany, children sing the *kalanda,* a carol similar to the ones they sing at Christmas and New Year's Eve. The second and most important 'Blessing of the Waters' takes place on the day of Epiphany, when the priest throws the Pastoral Cross into the sea, river or nearby reservoir. (In the large towns this ceremony takes on an official character and is attended by the State authorities.) As soon as the priest throws the cross into the water, young men dive to find it. Today it is more usual for a rope to be tied to the Cross first, as many were never retrieved! If the ceremony takes place in a harbour, all the boats lying at anchor, from passenger ships to the smallest rowing boat, are decked with bunting. The moment the

Cross is thrown into the water, the steamships sound their klaxons and the church bells begin to ring. Holy water from the church is taken back home and drunk by each member of the family.

Monastery of Dionysios, Mount Athos, founded in 1389, burned down in 1535, and rebuilt in 1547. Its library contains religious writings dating from the seventh century.

Midwife's Day, 8 January

A special celebration, called Midwife's Day, takes place at Moniktissia in northern Greece and at Petra, a village in Thrace on 8 January — St Dominic's Day. This is a special festival to honour the midwife or *Babo* of the village.

78

This is a day for women — the men stay indoors while their wives celebrate with food and wine. Although it is a minor feast in Greece, it has many interesting customs attached to it. Only women who are of child-bearing age are allowed to take part. They bring the midwife gifts which may be of use to her in her profession, and wash her hands, anticipating the day when she will assist them in childbirth. The midwife, adorned with gilded flowers, onion and garlic tresses, necklaces of dried figs, currants and carob beans, and one large onion instead of a watch, sits proudly upon a makeshift throne watching the scene with satisfaction.

After the midwife has given them her blessing, the women procede to elect a woman prime-minister and a ministerial council who are in power for twenty-four hours. The prime-minister reads the order of the day in front of the assembly; the two main points are:

1. It is forbidden for all women to stay at home or to return home before dawn, unless there is a sick person to be taken care of.
2. Any man who is seen outside the house — where he must stay, taking care of the household and the children — will be stripped by the women and drenched with cold water.

The second part of the celebration is the preparation of the night's banquet where the singing of indecent songs, dances and much drinking take place!

The third part of the celebration starts after sunset and lasts until sunrise. During the night, all the women gather in the cafés eating, drinking and singing with Dionysic zeal. After the feast, the midwife, still heavily bedecked, is led on a cart through the streets of the village to the public fountain where she is sprinkled with water. The feast is very similar to the ancient Dionysiac celebrations, like the *Thesmorphories* of Athens, reserved only for women. It has the same characteristics: fertility symbolism, consumption of wine and dancing.

Carnival

Carnival in Greece, as in other countries, is a time of gaiety and merrymaking. Before entering the long, austere period of Lent, during which the good Christian must keep a strict fast, it is natural that one should feel the need to enjoy oneself as much as possible. Above all Carnival means eating and drinking.

The Carnival season lasts three weeks. The first week, during which the fatted pigs are killed, is known as *Profoni* (coming from the Greek verb *profono,* to announce). The second week is known as the 'Meat Week'. The third week, called 'Cheese Week' is, in a way, an introduction and preparation for the Lent fast. The Thursday of the second week is called *Tsiknopempti* and is a really festive day. Even the poorest man will cook some meat over the fire and savour the good smell of grilled meat.

Masquerades are a very popular custom during Carnival. The masqueraders are most commonly called *maskarades,* from the word mask or *karnavaloi,* from the word carnival.

In Athens, in the old days, and to a lesser degree today, professional mummers visited the poor quarters of the city and danced around a maypole or a camel (no longer seen in Greece) ridden by a man dressed in a special costume. These burlesque processions were inevitably followed by a crowd of noisy children. In large towns, Carnival dances are held either at home or in dance-halls. Parades of masqueraders and carnival carts are organised by local committees.

The masqueraders often dress up as a wedding group, including the bride and groom, the old match-maker, the best man and the ash man. The ash man is dressed in the white-pleated skirt of national costume with bells around his waist and a small bag filled with ash to defend the bride and groom. The general gaiety of Carnival, the dancing and masquerading reach their highest points on the last Sunday of the Cheese Week.

In northern Greece, and especially in western Macedonia, it is the custom on the evening of Cheese Sunday to light bonfires in the village square. The children of Vogatsiko, in western Macedonia, prop up a small, thick-leafed tree in the ground and wrap dry branches and straw around its trunk so that it will make exploding noises when it is lit. At dusk the villagers sing and dance around the burning tree. When the flames begin to subside, all the single men in the village leap over the fire, calling out the name of the girl they fancy.

The evening meal on Cheese Sunday is a festive occasion. On the island of Karpathos, all the villagers take part in a meal at the mayor's house. The traditional dishes on this occasion are macaroni, eggs, cheese-pie, and a special dish called *tyrozoumi,* made of stewed wild herbs mixed with goat cheese. The last dish of the Cheese Sunday meal is usually eggs. On the island of Skyros and

(Opposite) *A typical Eclissaki (small church) near Elounda, Crete. This is one of the thousands of places of worship in Greece used on only a few occasions each year.*

other places, the last egg of the meal is hung from the ceiling by a string; the guests sitting around the table hit at the egg with their foreheads (hoping it does not break) to make it swing; they then try to catch it with their lips. This meal is usually followed by singing and dancing. The pepper dance is a favourite, the steps being danced with comical gestures.

There are strange beliefs attached to Cheese Sunday. If an ant or other insect is seen crawling under the table after the meal is over, it is a sign of prosperity. In Skyros, a person who sneezes during the evening meal will not outlive the year. In order to prevent this evil fate, the sneezer's shirt is torn open from the throat to the waist! (I suppose a lady would never sneeze!)

The last Sunday of Carnival is followed by Shrove Monday, or Green Monday, the first day of Lent. The Greek term *Kathari Deftera* or Clean Monday derives not only from the housewives' custom of cleaning their pots and pans with hot water mixed with ashes, but also because this day marks the beginning of their spiritual and bodily purification from the sins committed during Carnival. Although Shrove Monday belongs to the Lent period, it is essentially a continuation of Carnival, and is a festive holiday throughout Greece. It is a day that symbolises the first meeting with spring, and all the festivities take place in the open-air. Each family makes for the fields or woods, taking large picnics with them. The children fly their kites, a very familiar sight on Shrove Monday.

Traditional dishes for this special day are taramosalata, salad and sea food. These are eaten with *lagana,* a flat, oval leaf of unleavened bread which is baked only on this special day.

Procession of the Swallows, 1 March

The first of March is the day for the beautiful custom of the Procession of the Swallows. At Metrae in Thrace, two children fill a basket with ivy leaves; they pass a rod through the handle, and at the end of the rod they attach a wooden effigy of a bird which has little bells hanging around its neck. Two children go from house to house with the basket singing:

'A swallow came to us — she sat on a bough and sweetly sang; March, good March — and ugly

(Opposite) *Lindos Castle, Rhodes.*

February, what if you grow sour, what if you grow
cross; — there will soon be a smell of summer — and
even if you bring snow — it will soon be spring.

And you, good housewife, go down to the cellar, bring
up some speckled eggs, bring a little hen, bring a little
bun. Come in, Joy. Come in, Health, for the masters,
for the mistress, for the children and the parents, and
all the good relatives.'

The housewife takes some ivy leaves from the children's basket
and puts them in her hen's nest, so that it may lay many eggs. She
then gives the children a few eggs, and they move on to another
house. Ivy is believed to have the power to transfer fertility and
health to hens and other animals. This custom is of very ancient
origin; the 'Song of the Swallow' has reached us through
Athenaeus, a Greek writer of the third century AD.

Lent

Lent is a period of fasting, appointed by the Church in memory of
Christ's forty days in the wilderness, and lasts for forty-eight days.
It starts with Shrove Monday and ends with Easter.
  The rules of the fast are very strict. It is forbidden to eat any
animal products. Meat, eggs, fish and milk products are forbidden
by the Church. On Wednesdays and Fridays and during the whole
week preceding Easter (Holy Week) even wine and olive oil are
excluded. There are still many Greeks, especially in the villages, who
faithfully adhere to these rules, even those concerning the first three
days of Lent which are the strictest of them all; no water or bread
are allowed. It is usually the women who keep this absolute three
day fast; they are greatly honoured by the other villagers, who show
their respect by setting a table for them with special dishes — walnut
cakes, bean soup and so on — and bring them gifts at the end of
their fast. All night prayer in church is a common practice during
Lent.

Easter

Palm Week
The week preceding Holy Week is Palm Week and is commonly
known as 'Dumb Week' as no service is held in church throughout
this period except on Friday evening.

On Palm Sunday palm leaves are woven into various shapes like small baskets, half-moons, stars, and most of all, crosses. After the service, the priest stands at the church door and hands each person a branch of laurel or myrtle called *Vaya* and a small cross woven in palm. They are taken home and kept as a protection against evil spirits.

Holy Week

This is a week of general mourning. Singing, music and dancing are strictly forbidden by the Church. In some parts of Greece the church bells remain silent throughout Holy Week.

On Maundy Thursday all work is suspended until after Easter. Only housework is permitted. This is the time when Easter eggs are dyed the traditional red giving Maundy Thursday its other name, Red Thursday. Apart from the dyed eggs, Maundy Thursday is also the day when the Easter buns must be baked. They are usually made with yeast and flour with a variety of spices added to the mixture. Before the buns are put in the oven, they are studded with red eggs and dried fruit and their tops decorated. However, in spite of these preparations, Maundy Thursday remains a sacred and austere occasion held in special honour by the Greek people.

Good Friday

Good Friday is a day of total fast. Nearly the whole day is spent in attending the 'Descent from the Cross' and the procession of the *Epitaphios,* Christ's Funeral. Every shop and office is closed and flags fly at half mast. ˙

Towards noon, when the 'Descent from the Cross' takes place, the women start decorating the 'pall' (a piece of gold-embroidered cloth) which covers the bier upon which the body of Christ, represented by an icon, is to be placed. Each family in the village sends their flowers for the decoration. All the flowers are woven into wreaths or gathered into small bunches and pinned onto the pall until it is virtually covered in flowers. As soon as the decorations are complete the congregation make their way to the church to venerate the *Epitaphios.* Young girls sprinkle the pall with lemon leaves and rose petals. The icon representing the body of Christ is laid on the pall and is kissed by each of the worshippers.

At nightfall the *Epitaphios* is carried out of the church and the funeral procession begins. The banners and the Cross come first, followed by the bier which is, in turn, followed by the priests. In some areas of Greece the villagers burn incense and light bonfires during the procession and sometimes an effigy of Judas is burnt.

Roasting the Easter lamb. It is rubbed with herbs and olive oil, turned regularly, and basted every half hour.

Easter Sunday

Easter Sunday is the most important and joyful festival of the Greek Orthodox Church; so important that even dying on this day is considered to be lucky.

Today it is a custom to hold the Easter Sunday service on Saturday night and to announce the Resurrection of the Lord at midnight. By Saturday evening the churches are brightly decorated with laurel and myrtle, and sprays of rosemary are scattered over the floor. Everyone wears new clothes or at least one new item. Special candles are bought for the children, decorated with white or blue ribbons, flowers and gold thread. It is custom for a young man to send his fiancée a decorated candle and a gift.

When the service begins, the church is dimly lit. Then the moment comes when the few lights are extinguished and the church is in total darkness symbolising the grave. Suddenly the door of the Sanctuary opens and the Priest appears, holding a lighted candle. He chants: 'Come ye partake of the never setting light and glorify Christ who is risen from the dead.' The congregation crowd around the candle to light their own candles. Lights are passed from one candle to the next until the whole church is ablaze with the new Light.

After the congregation has lit their candles, the Priest leaves the church followed by the people. Outside he recites the Gospel passage
describing the Resurrection. Finally he calls *Christos anesti,* Christ is risen and everyone joins in *Christos anesti, Christos anesti.* The reply is *Alithos anesti,* He is risen indeed!

After the service has ended the people make their way home holding the lighted candle. It is a good omen if the holy light does not go out and is successfully taken into the house.

That evening the family share a late supper consisting of *Magiritsa,* a lamb and rice soup flavoured with dill, green salad with sardines and cheese pies. It is at this meal that the red eggs are eaten.

Easter Sunday lunch always consists of spit-roasted lamb. In every town and village the smell of roasting lamb pervades the air. In some provincial towns like Amfissa, Lamia, Arahova, and Levadia, spits are placed in rows in the main square and every visitor can taste the roasted lamb. The spit is turned slowly and the meat basted regularly with a mixture of oil, lemon and oregano.

The Spring Festival, 1 May

The first day of May is celebrated in Greece as a festival of spring. Everyone goes into fields or gardens to gather flowers to make a wreath. This wreath, which in large towns can be bought at the florists, is hung over the front door of the house. The farmers use green plants and fruit to make their wreaths. They always include garlic for protection against the evil eye and a thistle for protection against their enemies.

At Ayiasso, on the island of Lesbos, families who have unmarried daughters weave a wild plant called *daemonaria* into their May wreath. It is hoped that possible suitors will lose their heads and marry their daughters! On the island of Corfu, it is the custom to carry a maypole around the streets. The maypole is made from a young cypress tree crowned with a wreath of wild flowers, fruit and green vegetables. The foliage of the tree is decorated with yellow daisies and other flowers and hung with silk handkerchiefs. The maypole is carried around the city or village by a group of young men.

It is strange that this happy month should give birth to dark superstitions. The month of May, it is said, is also strewn with dangers. One should not cut material for clothing or marry during this month; nor is it wise to travel. Inevitably many of the old

Off to work in the countryside. Women still play a major role in the agricultural life of modern Greece.

superstitions are dying, but in some of the outlying villages, they linger still.

Harvest Time, June

June is the month devoted to the harvest, when the farmers are busy in their fields, as there is much work to be done. For this reason they do not have time for much celebration — the rituals are reserved for the first and last days of the harvest.

On the island of Skyros, the harvest begins as follows: a large stone is placed before a furrow in the field; the farmer makes the sign of the Cross over it three times, saying: 'May the grain and we, the reapers, be as strong as this stone.' There are several other customs believed to lighten the reaper's work. Wheatstalks from the first two sheaves are taken and stuck into the back of the reaper's belt so that his spine will not grow stiff with stooping. A handful of herbs is added to the first harvest meal, always a pie, to give strength to the reapers.

In Messinia, at the end of the harvest, the last standing wheat is called 'the ploughman's beard', meaning the farmer's beard. The reapers carry the farmer on their shoulders and refuse to put him down until he has promised everyone a feast of chicken and wine.

On the island of Lesbos, when two adjacent fields are being harvested it is the custom for the reapers to compete with each other. The men who finish first will, as they say, 'hunt the hare in the neighbour's field'. The winners also believe that their victory will make their crops more abundant next year.

Threshing Time, July

July is the time when Greek farmers thresh their wheat. In the mountainous villages where modern machines are still not used, the threshing is done by horses or oxen trampling over the wheat on the threshing floor. They move in circles, secured by a rein attached to a central pole. There are a number of customs associated with the start of threshing, and even more attached to the end of it.

On the island of Skyros, before they begin to thresh the wheat, the richer farmers ask the priest to hold a short service in the fields; the threshers who are to start work on that day must be spotlessly clean. At Lassithi, in Crete, when the threshing is over, the threshers gather the grain in a large heap, make the sign of the Cross over it and stand round in a circle. Then they stick a shovel into the mound, handle down, and bow three times. Taking a handful of grain they bow again, and throwing the grain over the shovel they kneel three times. They only begin to sack the grain once this ceremony has taken place.

Christmas

Christmas in Greece is still a religious celebration rather than the festive holiday that most of Europe has now adopted. This purely religious aspect of Christmas is not without its strange customs, which centre around the Christmas table and hearth. Several of the customs are very similar to those of New Year's Day. From the middle of the fourth century AD, 25 December was not only appointed Christ's birthday but also was made the first day of the year. This is why Christmas has taken so many of the Roman New Year customs which have survived to this day, even though 1 January has since been made the start of the year.

Early in the morning on Christmas Eve, the children take to the streets to sing the Christmas carols called *kalanda*. The *kalanda* are usually sung by young boys who accompany themselves on small drums and triangles and go from house to house singing and wishing every one health and prosperity. They are rewarded by buns, chestnuts, walnuts and sometimes money.

The main preparations for Christmas centre around the Christmas table. Every housewife will bake a *Christopsomo* — literally translated to mean 'Christ Bread'. It is a large sweet loaf with the family's own personal markings stamped on the top; a farming family, for example, would stamp the bread with a plough. The table is laid on Christmas Eve. The housewife first lays out the *Christopsomo* and a pot of honey; then she places dried fruit and nuts around them.

On Christmas morning the people go to morning Mass, as early as five o'clock, and it is usual for the children to be dressed in new clothes for this occasion. Roast pork is the traditional Christmas lunch although today, particularly in the cities, turkey is favoured.

Pouring oil or wine over the hearth is also a common custom in the villages. This can be traced to the ritual libations to the hearth made by the ancient Greeks in honour of their goddess Hestia, the goddess of the home.

TEN

Music and dance

For the Greek people, the joy of dancing is an integral part of life. It is difficult to trace the beginnings of dancing but it is thought that the Dionysic ritual of dancing around the altar could have been the origin of modern dancing in Greece. In the great tragedies of Aeschylus, Sophocles and Euripides, the chorus circled the stage.

Today both men and women enjoy dancing and with the right combination of food, wine, music and good company, there will always be dancing. Festivals, weddings, births, baptisms and holidays are only a few of the occasions when people dance, either in the home, the village square or, of course, the taverna. An opportunity for celebration is never missed!

Dances

Some of the well known dances are listed, but each of them is open to different interpretations, from one person to another or from one region to another.

The boulas

These are a series of carnival dances, performed in 2/4 time by men masquerading as women or wearing *fustanellas,* a sort of dress. The front of the bodice is covered with coins, which make a lot of noise when the dancer leaps up and down holding a sword. Some of the movements in the *boulas* acquired special significance during the Turkish occupation. It is said that the raising of the sword was the symbolic oath of freedom.

The syrtos

It is thought that this, the oldest of the dances, dates from the time of the ancient Greeks, when it was performed around the altar

An outbreak of spontaneous zembiko!

during sacred rituals. The joining of hands and the formation of an unbroken circle can be seen on many classical vases, and there are numerous frescoes in monasteries depicting the *syrtos,* with the lead dancer holding a handkerchief in his hand. The *syrtos* is danced in 2/4 time.

The kalamatianos
This is a kind of *syrtos,* only it is faster and more energetic and is danced in 7/8 time.

The tsakonikos
Danced in Tsakonia, the southern part of the Peloponnese, this one has deep roots in ancient history. It is danced in 5/4 or in 5/8 time, with the dancers holding each other tightly by the arm. Legend tells us that the *tsakonikos* represents Theseus's escape from the labyrinth at Knossos, in Crete.

The sousta
This is danced mainly in Crete and in the Dodecanese islands. It is danced in 2/4 time.

The mechanic
Sung and danced by the sponge divers, this dance was created by them. These divers frequently suffered paralysis from the effects of high water pressure and this dance symbolises the afflicted diver's attempt to dance; falling down, getting up again, and courageously continuing. The song which accompanies the *mechanic* is a very sad one.

The pendozalis
It is a war dance in 2/4 time and was danced by armed men until quite recently. It is a circular dance where the dancers hold each other by the shoulder. The lead dancers improvise spectacular steps and movements.

The zembekiko
It is a dance performed by one or two people, usually men, dancing opposite each other. This is danced in 9/8 time and is very popular in the islands.

The hasapiko
This very old dance was performed by butchers in the Byzantine era. The dancers, usually two to six people, dance in a straight line,

placing their arms across each others' shoulders. There are many variations on the steps and it is usually left to the dancers to perform their own interpretation within the basic form of the dance.

Musical instruments

All regions have their own variety of instruments. Usually the music for the dances and songs is based on the *ziyia* or small orchestra, comprising clarinette, violin, lute and *santouri*. Occasionally the *daouli* or drum is added, and sometimes a tambourine, flute or *pipiza* may be used.

In Crete, the lyre and the lute are played exclusively, with the lyre being played in a unique manner. The lyre player usually rests his foot on a stool and then sets up his lyre on his knees. Instead of pressing his fingers above the strings, he plays underneath the strings as though he were plucking them with his fingernails.

The people of Pontos generally play the lyre, but on certain occasions they play the bagpipes and sometimes the tambourine. The lyre is held and played vertically to enable the musician to move freely among the dancers.

The *hasapiko* and *zembekiko* are usually accompanied by the *bouzouki*, which is a modern, amplified version of the lute. The small *baglama*, or miniature *bouzouki*, is also used in these dances.

There are several Greek instruments which have evolved from the lyre, so often seen on the painted vases of classical Greece. Originally it developed into the *psalterion*, which is used in church music, and then gradually assumed the form of the *santouri*, as well as the *kanonaki*.

The *pipiza* is a member of the oboe family and, together with the *zourna*, has such a penetrating sound that it is usually played out of doors.

ELEVEN

Places of interest

Sounion

This majestic cape overlooking the blue water of the Saronic gulf was a perfect choice on which to build a temple of Poseidon, god of the sea. Here seafarers would make their sacrifices to ensure a safe journey before setting out into the more treacherous waters of the archipelago. The temple was destroyed by the Persians in 480 BC but rebuilt about 440 BC by Pericles, as were many other shrines throughout Attica.

On a lower hill, and beyond the fortifications of the Peloponnesian war, is the temple of Athena Sounias. It is a simple rectangle; Ionian colonnades were later added on two sides.

Cape Sounion is particularly beautiful at sunset.

Old Corinth

The temple of Apollo at Corinth is one of the oldest in Greece dating from around 580 BC. Corinth was, in classical times, a rich and famous trading centre. The Corinthians were renowned for their sculpture and art, but as Athens climbed towards its Golden Age, Corinth began to decline and its commerce passed into the hands of the Athenians. It prospered again when Philip II of Macedonia came to power, but in 146 BC, when Rome conquered Greece, it was razed to the ground and its magnificent treasures plundered.

In 44 BC, Julias Caesar built a new city on the ruins of the old and it soon became the seat of the Roman proconsul of Achaea in northern Peloponnese. St Paul came to Corinth to preach the Christian message in 51-52 AD and the city played an important part in the expansion of Christianity.

The Temple of Poseidon, Sounion, where sea-travellers offered a last sacrifice to the mighty god of the sea. Ancient Athens depended on its ships for power and prosperity.

Nauphlia

According to legend, Nauphlia was founded by Nauplios, son of Poseidon. One of his descendants, Palamides, invented the lighthouse and various measures and scales, and it is also thought that he introduced additional letters to the alphabet. Another explanation is that Nauphlia simply means 'place of ships'.

Today Nauphlia is an attractive town maintaining its local character with many fine old houses and shady courtyards, in quaint old streets. The Venetian castle of Palamides towers above the town and is reached by climbing 999 steps. It was built in 1714 by Lascelle, a year before the Turkish invasion. After the War of Independence in 1821, Nauphlia was made the capital of liberated Greece by Otho of Bavaria, the first king of modern Greece. A year later the capital was transferred to Athens.

Delphi

Here was the very heart of religious life in classical Greece. The shrine of Apollo, set in incredibly beautiful countryside, was where the Pythia held their seances. This was the famous oracle of Delphi. The Python, selected by the priests, claimed occult powers and it was through her that Apollo was supposed to speak. Usually her prophecies were plain common sense and she frequently discouraged acts of vengeance. The reconstruction of the procedure for consulting the oracle has been attempted by historians and archaeologists.

Visitors came from all over the known world to consult the priestess over problems ranging from military strategy to politics.

She received her visitors sitting on a three-legged stool while they stood bare headed before her. On the floor, in front of her, was a small rounded mount called the *omphalos* representing the centre of the world. A fire made of laurel and other herbs created a pungent smoke which filled the room. It has been suggested that the smoke may have had a narcotic effect on the Pythia if it was inhaled deeply.

During the Persian war the oracle was consulted regularly. The Pythia informed the delegation that they would be safe within their wooden walls, referring to their ships. The Greeks won a decisive naval battle at Salamis, thus justifying their faith in the oracle.

Also at Delphi is the Tholos, a rare circular temple built in marble in the fourth century BC. Its purpose is unknown.

The Acropolis, Athens

The Acropolis, which means 'high city', is a rocky hill dominating the centre of Athens. Here you can find the most famous buildings of Classical Greece: the Parthenon, the Erecthecum, the Propylaea and the temple of Athena Nike.

The Parthenon, Acropolis, Athens, built between 447 and 432 BC.

The Parthenon

It was built on the highest part of the Acropolis in the Golden Age of Pericles, in the fifth century BC. The architects were Ictimus and Callicrates, and the ornamentation was the work of Phidias, who also co-ordinated the whole plan. The Doric structure was built of pure marble from nearby Mount Pentelicus and consisted of two rooms. In one stood the huge statue of Athena the Virgin, made by Phidias in gold and ivory around a wooden core, and in the other were the treasures of the temple, including Xerxes's silver-footed throne on which he had sat and watched his forces defeated at Salamis.

The Erectheum

Built between 421-406 BC, it is basically a rectangle with three porches at different levels and, inside, two sanctuaries, one dedicated to Poseidon Erectheus and the other to Athena Polias. The south porch has six statues of beautiful maidens supporting it, like columns. In the area of the Erectheum are found the oldest and most sacred relics of ancient Athens: the Mycenaean palace, the tomb and shrine of Kekrops, the mark of Poseidon's trident, and the sacred olive tree of Athena.

The Propylaea

This monumental gate was built between 437 and 432 BC on the site of an older Propylaea which had been destroyed by the Persians. It was designed by the architect Mnesicles but was never quite completed because of the outbreak of the Peloponnesian war. On the right of the Propylaea, on a high platform, stands the beautiful little temple of Athena Nike, or Wingless Victory, built in the fifth century to commemorate the Greek victories over the Persians.

The ancient Agora, Athens

The Agora was the market place and civic, social and religious centre of Athens, dating from the sixth century BC. Here the law courts, state offices, public archives, gymnasium and shops were found. It was here, too, that the great orators expounded their views. Under the long colonnades, which gave summer shade and winter shelter, Socrates and Plato taught their pupils. The Agora was rebuilt by Attalus, King of Pergamum, in the second century BC, as a tribute to Athens where he had received his education.

The Temple of Hephaestos, Athens

This temple bounds the Agora on the west side and was built in the fifth century BC. It was designed by Ictimus the brilliant architect co-responsible for the Parthenon. This is the best preserved Greek temple, with its 34 columns still supporting the original roof. It was dedicated to Hephaestos, god of blacksmiths and potters.

The Theatre of Herodus Atticus, Athens

Sitting at the foot of the Acropolis, this theatre was built in 161 AD by Herodus Atticus, a wealthy friend of the emperor, Hadrian. The theatre, seating 5,000 people, was expertly restored and is used today for the summer festival of music and drama.

The Theatre at Epidaurus

This is the best preserved of all Greek theatres and dates from the fourth century BC. It seats 14,000 people and is still used for the annual summer festival of drama, held in July and August. The acoustics are so perfect that every word spoken by the actors is audible at the back of the theatre, some 55 rows away. (It takes about 1½ hours to drive to Epidaurus from Athens. If you are attending a performance, I suggest you take a cushion or something soft to sit on.)

Crete

Crete is the largest of the Greek islands and was inhabited from the Neolithic period. The life that developed on the island from 2800 to 1100 BC was truly amazing. The Minoans, a lively and intelligent people, were superb artists and ingenious architects. They lived in magnificent surroundings, without fortifications, in prosperity and peace. The first palace of Knossos, built around 2000 BC, is a tangible reminder of their brilliance. They were well advanced in engineering skills and were able to level large areas of land to build Knossos and Phaistos, another city on the other side of the island. They imported copper from Cyprus and gold from Sinai and Nubia. Their works of art, jewellery and implements can be seen at the Museum in Heraklion.

*Knossos (*above*), five kilometres from Heraklion, Crete, inhabited for nearly five thousand years, was the home of the legendary King Minos. Heraklion's attractive Venetian harbour (*below*) is where the daily ferry boats arrive.*

Inside the walls of the old Crusader's castle in Rhodes town (**above**) *are shops, restaurants, churches, mosques and museums.* (**Below**) *A peaceful little cove at Lindos, Rhodes.*

A hieroglyphic script was developed and an incredible example of this, the Phaestos Disc, can be seen in the museum at Heraklion. It has not, as yet, been deciphered.

About 1700 BC a great catastrophe occurred, probably an earthquake, which destroyed the palaces. They were quickly rebuilt and can be seen today.

The walls were decorated with beautiful frescoes and paintings, and an elaborate plumbing and drainage system was built. Large spaces were allocated for the storage of grain showing the prosperity of the city. The enormous storage jars can still be seen at Knossos. Around 1450 BC, another major catastrophe occurred. It is thought that this was the result of the volcanic explosion on Thera, or Santorini, to the north. It is possible that an earthquake followed, destroying all the major sites on the island. Only at Knossos did partial recovery take place and the great palace entered its final phase around 1450 to 1300 BC.

In 1150 BC, the island was conquered by the Dorians and by the eighth century BC Crete was a flourishing Dorian island and excelled once more artistically.

Rhodes

Rhodes is the largest of the Dodecanese (meaning twelve) islands. The Greeks first made their appearance in the Mycenaean period about 1500 BC. After the Dorians landed on the island about 1100 BC, three great centres developed at Ialysos, Kameiros and Lindos. These three cities minted their own coins in the sixth and fifth centuries BC, a sign of prosperity and commercial success. Lindos, on the south-east coast of Rhodes, was the ancient capital of the island before the town of Rhodes was founded. The temple of Athena crowns a gigantic rock which rises directly from the sea and stands within the walls of a Frankish castle.

The mighty Colossus, one of the seven wonders of the ancient world, straddled the entrance to the harbour of Rhodes. It was 30 metres high and, erected in 290 BC, it was destroyed by an earthquake in 227 BC.

In 1306, the chief admiral of the Byzantine empire sold Rhodes to the military Order of St John of Jerusalem which was, at that time, established in Cyprus after its losses in Palestine. The Order was organised into national subdivisions: Provence, Auvergne, France, Italy, England, Germany, Castille and Aragon, and it was ruled by a Grand Master. Rhodes was fortified by the Order and resisted several Turkish attacks. However, the island finally surrendered to Suleiman the Magnificent in 1522, and the Order of St John retired to Malta.

Kos

Kos is one of the most beautiful Dodecanese islands and was the birthplace of Hippocrates, the father of medicine. The island was, and still is, renowned for its healing water. The people of Kos

The Asklepeion, Kos, dedicated to Asklepios, the god of healing.

worshipped Asklepios, the god of healing, and dedicated one of its most important sanctuaries, the Asklepeion, to him. It was built in the fourth century BC on a site providing the necessary peaceful surroundings. The Dorian temple of Asklepios was built at the top of a great stairway leading down to a lower terrace where the god's altar stood. On the third terrace, which was the main treatment area, there were arcades with rooms, sulphur springs and sacred places for votive offerings. Lower still, the baths and cistern were found.

The old city of Kos was destroyed in the Peloponnesian war and the new city was founded in 366 BC. It quickly prospered and became one of the greatest maritime centres of the Aegean. In 142 BC, it was destroyed again by an earthquake, built and destroyed again in 469 AD, rebuilt and almost destroyed yet again in 554 AD, after which the inhabitants abandoned the city!

Alexander the Great occupied the island in 336 BC and, on his death, it passed into the hands of Philadelphus, who was born on the island. Philadelphus became the second pharaoh of the Ptolemy dynasty who ruled over Egypt from the death of Alexander the Great to its eventual conquest by Rome in the reign of Cleopatra.

Today, in the new town of Kos, there stands a giant plane tree. The trunk is 1.5 metres in diameter and its branches are propped up by ancient marble fragments. It is said that Hippocrates lectured under the shade of its branches, but in reality the tree is no more than 500 years old.

The Castle of the Knights is the town's chief monument, and was built from 1391-96. The castle has two enclosures, one within the other, and is entered by a drawbridge and gateway. Parts of the castle were built with stone from the Asklepeion.

Some of the inhabitants of Kos are Muslim and the remainder mostly orthodox Christians.

Delos

Delos is the smallest island of the Cyclades and was once the religious and political centre of the Aegean. It was the birth-place of Apollo and his sister Artemis. It prospered in the fifth century BC when it was the treasury for the Athenian League, but after the treasury was removed to Athens by Pericles, its decline was inevitable. In 426 BC the Athenians ordered the island to be purified and this meant that no births or deaths were allowed on the sacred island. If this happy or unhappy event was about to take place, the person was quickly removed to nearby Rhenaea, another small island separated from Delos by a narrow strip of water.

By the end of the fourth century BC, Delos was independent and came under the influence of Egypt. Many trade routes passed through Delos instead of Piraeus and for the next 150 years, it enjoyed prosperity. Many pilgrims came to visit the sacred shrines and created a busy trade centre.

The famous lions of Delos were sculptured in the seventh century BC from marble imported from the nearby island of Naxos. They were placed near the Sacred Lake to guard the city.

Pella

The birthplace of Philip II of Macedonia in 382 BC, and also his son Alexander the Great in 356 BC, Pella was the capital of Macedonia and an important artistic and literary centre. It is famous for its mosaics.

TWELVE

So you want to speak Greek?

Whenever visiting a foreign country, it is always helpful to be able to speak a little of the language. I have chosen a few phrases for you which will be useful, but accept no responsibility for knotted tongues and sore larynges! It may be difficult to believe, but over twelve per cent of the words in the English language are directly derived from Greek roots.

Stress

The Greek language is purely phonetic, every letter in each word is pronounced. It is important that the stress is placed on the correct part of the word. For example, confusion could arise with the word *taxí*, which means motor taxi when the stress (denoted by the accent) is on the final letter; but if the stress is placed on the first syllable — *táxi* — it means 'class' or 'order'.

Pronunciation

a as in hat
o as in hot
e as in bet
x is pronounced as ks
t is pronounced as d

u as in pull
i as in sit
ou as in lute
d is pronounced as th

Useful words and phrases

Excuse me   *Me sighoríte*
Sorry   *Signómi*

105

How are you?	*Tíkánis?*
Good	*Kalá*
Thank you	*Efharistó*
Where are you from?	*Apó pou ísthe?*
Do you speak English?	*Miláte Anglicá?*
I do not speak Greek	*Den miló Eliniká*
It does not matter	*Den pirázzi*
Hello/Goodbye	*Yássas*
Good morning	*Kaliméra*
Good afternoon	*Hérete*
Good evening	*Kapispéra*
Good night	*Kaliníkta*
Yes	*Ne*
No	*Óhi*
May I? or Can I?	*Mboró?*
Please/Don't mention it	*Parakaló*
Hot	*Zestó*
Cold	*Krió*
Tomorrow	*Ávrio*
Today	*Símera*
Morning	*Proí*
Noon	*Messiméri*
Night	*Vrádi*
Tonight	*Apópse*
I don't understand	*Den katalavéno*
Safe journey	*Kaló taxíthi*

Travel and directions

How far is the railway station/bus station/bus stop/airport?	*Pósso makriá íne ostathmós trénou/ leoforíou/stassis leoforíou/ do aerodrómio?*
What time is the next	*Ti óra íne toepómenon trénon/*
train/bus/aeroplane/ferry	*leoforíou/aeropláno/karávi.*
I want a taxi please	*Thélo éna taxí parakaló.*
How much will it cost, roughly, from here to the centre?	*Póssa perípou tha stikhísi apó edó sto kéntron?*
I have lost my ticket	*Ékhasa toissitírio mou.*
How much is the fare to ...	*Pósso ékhi toissitírio ya ...*
Single ticket	*Apló issitírio*

106

Return ticket	*Issitírio alleretoúr*
Please take me to ...	*Párteme sto ..... parakaló*
Is the Acropolis very far from here?	*Íne makriá i Akrópolis ap edó?*
Do you know where the hotel is?	*Xérete pou íne to xenodohíon?*

Eating out

Do you have a menu?	*Ékhete menú?*
Can you recommend a good taverna?	*Mvoríte na mou sistísete mía kalí tavérna?*
Is service included?	*Íne mazí ke dofilothórima?*
The bill please	*Ton logariasmó parakaló*
I think the bill is wrong	*Nomízo o logariasmós íne láthos*
Wine — white/red/rosé	*Krassí — áspro/kókkino/rosé*
Do you have fresh fish?	*Éhete frésko psári?*
I want the meat very well cooked/medium/rare	*Thélo to kréas polí kalopsiméno/métria/polí ligopsiméno.*
I don't want garlic/onions octopus/oil	*Den thélo skórtho/kremíthia/ octapóthi/láthi*
One cup of tea with milk please	*Éna tsaí me gála, parakaló*
May I have a coffee/ice cream	*Mboró naého éna kafé/pagotó?*

At the bank and post office

Where is the nearest bank?	*Poú íne i pió kontiní trápeza?*
May I have change for this note?	*Mboró na ékho psilá yaftó tokhartonómisma?*
Where is the post office?	*Pou íne to takhithromío?*
I want to send a telegram	*Thélo na stílo éna tilegráfima*

Emergencies

Where is the nearest police station	*Pou íne opió kontinós astinomikós stathmós?*
There has been an accident	*Sinévike thistíkhima*
Please will you call a doctor?	*Parakaló kaléste éna yadró?*

| Where is the nearest hospital? | *Pou íne do pió kontinó nosokomío?* |
| Quick, someone is drowning! | *Grígora kápios pnígete!* |

Numbers
One	*Éna*
Two	*Dío*
Three	*Tría*
Four	*Téssera*
Five	*Bénte*
Six	*Éxi*
Seven	*Eptá*
Eight	*Octó*
Nine	*Ennéa*
Ten	*Déka*
Fifteen	*Déka bénte*
Twenty	*Íkossi*

Days of week
Sunday	*Kiriakī*
Monday	*Theftéra*
Tuesday	*Tríti*
Wednesday	*etárti*
Thursday	*Pémpti*
Friday	*Paraskeví*
Saturday	*Sávaton*

Months
January	*Ianouários*
February	*Fevrouários*
March	*Mártios*
April	*Aprílios*
May	*Máios*
June	*Ióunios*
July	*Ióulios*
August	*Ávgoustos*
September	*Septémvrios*
October	*Octóvrios*
November	*Noémvrios*
December	*Thekémvrios*

Daily boat trips from Piraeus visit Hydra in the Saronic Gulf.

THIRTEEN

Artistic events

The National Tourist Organisation of Greece presents the following
artistic events throughout the year:

The Athens Festival

Drama, opera, music and ballet make up the programme of the
Athens Festival which is offered to spectators who throng the
Herodus Atticus Odeon. It is an artistic programme performed by
Greek and foreign artists. (July-September)

The Epidaurus Festival

The *Epidavria* are a series of performances of ancient Greek drama,
presented in the ancient open-air theatre at Epidaurus. The
performances given here are considered to be among the best in the
world. (July-August)

The Philippi and Thassos Festival

Ancient drama performances are given in the ancient theatres at
Philippi and on the island of Thassos. (July-August)

Dodonaea

Performances of ancient drama are given in the ancient theatre at
Dodoni during August.

Lycabettus

Various artistic performances are given during the summer season in the open-air theatre on the Lycabettus (Likavitos) hill in Athens. (Mid-June to the end of August)

Son et lumière

From early April to end of October, *Son et Lumière* performances are given in Athens, Corfu and Rhodes in several foreign languages.

Film and light music festivals

As part of the Thessaloniki International Trade Fair (mid-September) and during the first week, a Festival of Greek Light Music is held in the Palais des Sports which is located inside the grounds of the Fair.

As soon as the Fair is over, two interesting festivals of Greek and foreign films are organised. Both events take place in the theatre of the Association of Macedonian studies. Also during the summer season, artistic events are organised in the theatre of the Dassos of Thessaloniki, which include ancient drama, opera and music.

The 'Demetria' Festival

As part of the broader programme which accompanies the Thessaloniki International Trade Fair, there is every October a series of theatrical, musical, ballet and operatic performances, given by Greek and foreign companies, as a revival of the tradition of Byzantine festive events in the capital of Macedonia.

Folk dancing

From May to September each year, there are performances of Greek dancing at the open-air theatre on the Filopappus hill in Athens, presented by the Dora Stratou song and ballet troupe, which is well-known throughout the world. From November to April, every Monday at the Aliki theatre in Athens, the Greek Lyceum gives presentation of Greek folk dances. Finally, on the island of Rhodes, from June to October every year, the Nelly Dimoglou troupe presents Greek folk dancing in the theatre of the old town of Rhodes and from November to May in the theatre at Rodini.

The Theatre

A classical and modern repertoire is presented in Athenian theatres all the year round. The two organised State theatrical companies, the National Theatre in Athens and the Northern Greece National Theatre at Thessaloniki, are committed to festival programmes organised by the Greek National Tourist Organisation every summer, but they present well-known plays by Greek and foreign playwrights during the winter.

The Lyric Theatre

Known in Greece as the *Lyriki Skini,* the Lyric Theatre presents operas at the Olympia theatre in Athens. The Lyriki Skini transfers its activities to the Herodus Atticus Odeon in summer, to participate in the Athens Festival.

Wine festivals

Every summer the National Tourist Organisation of Greece organises two wine festivals where a Dionysian atmosphere can be found.

In Athens
This takes place in the grove and tourist pavilion at Dafni, eleven kilometres from the city, from 14 July to 9 September. A large variety of Greek wines are available at no charge. Three self-service tavernas are also open, offering typical Greek specialities. There is dancing and singing and everyone is welcome.

In Alexandroupolis
The festival takes place in the grounds of the National Tourist Organisation's camping site from 7 July to 19 August. Again the wines drunk are free and like the Dafni festival there are tavernas for self-service food.

Index

Page references to photographs appear in **bold** type

114